T0131531

SHARE MY RIDE

ARCHIE C. EDWARDS

 iUniverse®

SHARE MY RIDE

iUniverse books may be ordered through booksellers or by contacting:

iUniverse
1663 Liberty Drive
Bloomington, IN 47403
www.iuniverse.com
1-800-Authors (1-800-288-4677)

Because of the dynamic nature of the Internet, any web addresses or links contained in this book may have changed since publication and may no longer be valid. The views expressed in this work are solely those of the author and do not necessarily reflect the views of the publisher, and the publisher hereby disclaims any responsibility for them.

Any people depicted in stock imagery provided by Getty Images are models, and such images are being used for illustrative purposes only. Certain stock imagery © Getty Images.

ISBN: 978-1-5320-7701-2 (sc)
ISBN: 978-1-5320-7700-5 (e)

Library of Congress Control Number: 2019908592

Print information available on the last page.

iUniverse rev. date: 06/27/2019

Dedication

This book is dedicated to all the rideshare drivers in the greater Nashville, TN area. Kudos to everyone who takes time out of their day to help passengers get from point A to point B.

Acknowledgments

I want to acknowledge my wife for giving me the time and money it took to bring this project into fruition. I want to thank my sisters for their involvement on this project. I want to thank Mini for inspiring me to take on this project. Finally, I want to thank my niece, Zoe, for providing me the illustrations used throughout this book.

Preface

I am sure by the time anyone reads this book; they are familiar with the idea of "rideshare". This is a concept where people are either scared to death of the filth and noxious fumes of your average taxicab, they don't own a car, they don't want to deal with parking, they intend to get drunk, or any number of reasons. So, they decide to take a chance by riding with everyday individuals like me in my personal vehicle. I want to clearly say that while I can be rather sarcastic, I am not a professional driver and I have never driven a cab.

However, I found myself out of work after walking away from a horrible, toxic company who will remain nameless, and therefore I needed to find a way to make some money as I searched for my next adventure. UBER and LYFT were practical money-making options when I was hunting for a job. I could drive whenever I wanted, go where I wanted, and I would be acting as my own boss which was rather appealing. The goal was to drive LYFT or UBER in the early morning, and then spend the afternoons searching the internet for potential jobs. This seemed like a good plan even though when driving with any rideshare company, the driver doesn't make as much money as one would expect. I should note that I drive an F-150 and a Ford Escape. From time to time I will refer to both as I have used both while out scouring the city for long-lost souls who need a ride to their destination.

The purpose of this book is not to slam the rideshare companies, but to give the reader a chance to see what rideshare is like from the perspective of the driver. The driver must absorb the cost of maintenance, gas, tire wear, taxes, and random accidents that can really set you back if you are not careful. I needed to ensure that

I was making some money each day, so a minimum number of rides was needed as well as providing the best customer service possible. Hopefully good customer service would increase my tips.

As I began to drive in the mornings, I averaged 10 – 12 rides each day. Most of them were rather uneventful. I spent most of my time driving passengers to the airport or to work. Occasionally I would pick up some high school kids who have absolutely zero concept of time and either sleep in late, miss their normal ride, or they miss the school bus. I often drove people home from work or the occasional eating establishment, and I do admit, I drove a few people home from their random "booty calls". I suspect these were "booty calls" but I didn't ever have the guts to ask and get all the juicy details. I did pick up one girl who gave me some of the details, but you will read about her later.

I will also tell you that I have worked in the customer service world my entire life. I spent my high school years working at Toys "R" Us which has since gone out of business. I spent my college years working at various restaurants which gave me plenty of insight into working with the general public. I learned quickly that people in restaurants have few manners when they eat and, in this day, and age, manners are few and far between. I would encourage you to go to a restaurant and as you are eating, just watch other people. It's pretty gross.

Later I spent a year working in the hotel business. I thought people were gross when they ate in a restaurant, but they do not compare to the disgusting mess most travelers leave in their hotel room when they check out. Next, I spent 16 years in the appliance industry, listening to sob stories every day from people about how appliances break. Customer's would think the manufacturers would give a warranty that says, "your appliance will last forever and is entirely indestructible, no matter how much you abuse it". But alas, that has not happened yet.

During all these years I have always thought about writing down the stories I encountered when dealing with basic customer service. Procrastination always got the better of me and while the idea was always there, it never formulated into anything tangible on paper. Then I started to drive people around in my truck and I could procrastinate no longer. As I started to drive from one destination to another, I began making notes about the adventures I seemed to be having.

All of the names in this book are fake. I honestly don't remember their names, but I remember the situations vividly and wrote about them within hours or days of each event. I don't spend time describing each person because mostly, I drive at night. Passengers ride in the backseat most of the time. I pay attention to the road and the rideshare app, therefore I really don't focus on faces. Most of the people in this book I could not pick out of a police line.

The stories in the book are real and in no specific order although for the sake of continuity, I tried to lump some of the stories together such as police related stories or stories that had to do with taking passengers to the airport. I have absolutely no reason to make up any facts because the truth is where the real humor can be found. I am quite certain that the passengers who rode in my truck will not remember nor will they self-identify with the fact that they gave me the material I would be using in this book. Some of them were simply too drunk to remember, others never stopped talking. One passenger never stopped looking in the mirror. Customers can be fun, interesting, obnoxious, and downright revolting. Anyone in customer service is probably nodding their head up and down as they read this.

Once again, the following stories are true stories from driving passengers in Nashville, Tn. Music City is an awesome tourist town and there is never a shortage of passengers who need help getting around the town. Some of these stories are funny, some of them are not. Some of them may even seem boring, but they will give you a good sense of what it's like for a rideshare driver. Some of them will make you laugh while others will simply make you scratch your head or shrug your shoulders. I also want to make note that every rideshare driver has stories to tell. Every driver must deal with the general public, and I am sure most of them have better stories than I have to tell, but the stories in the book happened to me to the best of my recollection. I have tried not to exaggerate the details, but I do make share some rather sarcastic comments which may make you laugh, or they may even offend you. If you are offended by sarcasm, you shouldn't have purchased this book.

Regardless of the story, there is always a take-home lesson to be learned. I haven't spelled out those lessons per se, but they are there. Lessons such as don't drink and drive, always use a car seat, don't bathe yourself in cologne are just some of the lessons the reader should surmise. Other lessons such as don't wear a bathing suit to work or don't leave your purse with a naked guy may not be so subtle. Either way, I hope you enjoy reading about the passengers who gave me all the crazy stories.

I have also included a section of the book called Lessons Learned for passengers and drivers. Often, I am asked questions from passengers who are thinking about becoming a rideshare driver. Therefore, I included some lessons and advice that would serve a new driver well. Then I included some tips for passengers. These are things they should know and consider before making that rideshare request. I hope the readers will find all the lessons and tips I have included to be helpful and comical.

1
THE TENT

I should begin these stories by telling everyone about the very first passenger I ever picked up in my truck while using the rideshare app. It was a Friday morning. I spent the afternoon on Thursday debating if rideshare was a practical way to make money and pass the time while I was job hunting. In fact, it was and so I downloaded the app, uploaded pictures of myself, my registration, my driver's license, and proof of insurance to my profile. I received word from both rideshare companies that everything had been approved and I was ready to go. I went to bed knowing that I would try out being a pseudo-cab driver in the morning.

Friday morning at 4:15 am, I got into my truck and turned on the heater. Then I turned on the rideshare app for the first time. I am not sure what I was thinking, but I remember wondering how long it would take before I got my first request and then wondered if I would know what to do even though I had worked thru all the tutorials online the night before. It took less than a minute and the accept ride button was blinking at me. Yay, I got my first ride request. I accepted the ride and headed off using the GPS within the app to show me the way.

Sadly, the first ride was at the building next door to the horrible company I had left a week prior. I didn't let that hold me back. I arrived and my first passenger got into the truck. She said, "Good morning, do you mind if we stop by the Circle-K so I can grab some snacks?"

At this point, I didn't know what else to say other than, "sure". We stopped and the passenger got some snacks and then we were on our way. I looked down and noticed that her stop was about 20 miles away which surprised me. We drove East and then North. That's about all I can say because we were out in the middle of nowhere. The roads were dark because no one in their right mind would put in streetlights out in the middle of nowhere.

Finally, we arrived at a campsite and I turned into the main drive as per my GPS. At this time, the passenger began giving me directions to turn this way and then that way, until we arrived at her tent. Yes, I had driven a woman from her job at 4:30 am to a tent, in the middle of nowhere. She got out, zipped herself up in the tent and the ride was over. I admit I had a few questions, but I never asked any of them before she got out.

The rest of the day was pretty good. I had 7 pick-ups for a total of $95 in a 4-hour time block. I headed home. The next morning, I got in my truck at 4:15 am and turned on the app. Again, it went off in 2 minutes time and my first ride of the day was the same lady who lived in the tent. This time I was not about to let her get away without asking her a ton of questions.

To make a long story short, the lady was camping that week to get away from her sister. She lived with her sister who had three children under the age of 5. That thought alone gave me a headache. She told me that sometimes she "just needed a break" and so she went camping...... with her cat! "Wait, what? You have a cat in your tent" I asked? She said the cat enjoyed camping. I'm wondering if the cat told her this. Sure enough, she would go to work each day and leave the cat zipped up in the tent which was in the middle of nowhere. She went on to tell me that the tent was insulated though she had a small heater that she rarely used. She loved the peace and quiet which I am assuming the cat enjoyed as well. So, two days in a row I drove a woman to a tent. I had figured I would be taking passengers to the airport or taking people to work, but instead I was taking people to their random campsites. This is when I knew I should begin to write down some of the stories I would encounter because in my best creative times I couldn't make up the stories that rideshare drivers encounter every day on the job.

The lady who lived in a tent with her cat...... meow!

2

THE MASSAGE THERAPIST

I am not one to judge, and I am only suspecting that the woman I picked up on a Saturday morning at 5:25 am was a woman of many talents. This happened on my second day as a rideshare driver. I had already finished two rides when I got a call from a very nice young lady named Sheila. I won't use her real name because she told me her name and where she works during the week. She said she was a massage therapist during the week at a local therapy office, somewhere in Nashville which is over 500 square miles. Again, I know the exact location but will keep that a secret as it's not relevant to the story.

Sheila was a beautiful blonde who walked to the truck wearing tight black jeans, white leather thigh-high boots with 4-inch heels, a white shirt, and a leopard print jacket. Very dressy for 5:25 am. I was taking her to a "friend's" house who lived in a gated community about 5 miles away. This was too far to walk in 4-inch heels. Oddly enough, she didn't really know much about her "friend" when I asked how long they have known each other. She said they were not dating. I joked and said, "maybe he will make you breakfast". Sheila replied in a sad voice, "I think I am his breakfast". This is where I learned to stop asking so many questions as I was not exactly ready for that answer at 5:25 am.

The friend ended up calling her and they got into a small quibble about numbers. I didn't ask if the numbers were house numbers, phone numbers, or financial numbers. I kept my mouth shut, dropped her off in the apartment complex and went on my way.

I have been to that complex over a dozen times and have thought about Sheila each and every time. I also think about Fred because that apartment complex must have one hundred speed bumps, and I hate every one of them.

3
AMY, TARA, AND THE NAKED GUY

This story is one of my favorites. I have done a ton of rides and I assure you; this is one that I will never forget. It was 3:23 am and I was sitting in front of Nathan's house when he canceled the ride. I got $5 for the cancellation and immediately was dispatched to pick up Amy who lived .4 miles away, only 2 minutes according to the rideshare app. While on my way, I got a text from Amy stating, "I'm going to need more than 2 minutes".

I figured, that when I arrive, the app starts a counter and a passenger has 5 minutes to come to the vehicle before they can be marked as a No Show. So, Amy had 5 minutes rather than 2. When I arrived, I sat out in front of the house which had a sidewalk leading to the front door. After 3 minutes, Amy walked out to the truck. Her hair was soaking wet and I could tell she just got out of the shower and threw on her clothes as fast as possible. She didn't have any shoes on, in fact, I am willing to bet she only had on a shirt and a pair of pants, nothing else. She opened the door and told me she would need 10 minutes and it was up to me if I wanted to wait. I told her I would gladly wait 10 minutes. She turned and disappeared back into the house.

8 minutes later, Amy came out to the truck. When she exited the house, she left the front door standing wide open. I mean, all the way open. I could see into the house which had a short staircase in full view. Amy got into the truck, thanked me for waiting, and told me that her friend would be right out. I could tell that Amy had found her shoes and her bra, both of which she put on in those 8 minutes.

2 minutes later, her friend Tara walked down the stairs with a naked guy walking behind her. He had a white towel in his hand which covered one leg and nothing else. He was simply walking around butt naked. Tara came to the truck only to realize she forgot her purse, so she went back into the house. Amy commented she didn't know where Tara hung her purse. I, in turn, commented that I knew of one place where the purse was not hanging.

2 minutes later, Tara walked down the stairs for the second time with the naked guy in close pursuit. She turned and began kissing naked guy while Amy and I made some rather interesting comments which I will leave out of this book. Tara then walked out to the truck as the naked guy stood in the doorway catching the night breeze. I suddenly had memories of my drill sergeants yelling, "Attention!"

As we headed to their destination, I asked them about their evening. As you can guess, the two ladies were in town for the weekend. They met two guys while they were out at the bar and they came back to their place for some recreational activity. I was right when I assumed Amy's shower was not a solo mission. The girls were in town with their 70-year old mother who wanted to visit Nashville. Their mother was back at their hotel room sleeping while they were seeing the sights that Nashville has to offer at 3:30 in the morning. We were halfway back to the hotel when Tara decided that she must have McDonald's and begged me to find one so she could have a McChicken.

Luckily, Nashville has a McDonalds on Broadway and we were able to stop and go through the drive-thru which was also rather comical. I pulled up and let Amy and Tara order their food from the rear driver side window. The person who was taking their order had a very odd accent, combined with a bad speaker system that can be found at half of the drive-thru's in America. The woman taking the order kept saying something that sounded like "Truth or Dare". That is what I heard, that is what Amy heard, and that is what Tara heard. When we pulled around, we asked the lady what she was saying. She told us she kept repeating $10.58 over and over. To this day I am still trying to figure out how to say $10.58 while making it sound like "truth or dare".

I finally got Amy and Tara back to their hotel. They handed me a $10 as a tip and they headed into their hotel, very thankful that I chose to wait for them as they finished in the shower and said goodbye to naked guy. I drove off and waited for my next dispatch.

15 minutes later I had picked up a girl named Felicity and was taking her home when I got a text message from Amy. "Have you seen Tara's Discover card?" I dropped off Felicity and then tried to respond to Amy's text message after checking the backseat with a flashlight. I didn't find Tara's credit card and I never heard from Amy or Tara again. I hope they had a great trip although visions of naked guy are burned into my brain. Some things can't be unseen. Perhaps the naked guy had her discover card?

4

MELANIE THE DANCER

Although I dislike my cell phone most of the time, I do enjoy the talk-to-text application. When I pick up a rider who has a story, I use the talk-to-text to send myself reminders or notes about the ride. After I dropped off Melanie, I sent myself 6 very long texts about the ride to remind me about all the crazy things this person told me in a short 17-minute ride from her place of employment to her home.

I decided to go out driving late at night for a change of pace. I left my house at 11 pm and planned to drive until 6 am. At 3 am, I received a call to pick up Melanie. When I arrived at the location, it was a gentleman's club with the word "Strippers" in bright neon lights on the side of the building. I would have guessed the place had "strippers", but their advertising department decided to take the guesswork out of the equation. After I arrived, Melanie came walking out the side door within 30 seconds. She was a petite, cute girl although I remember thinking to myself, "she looks like an average college kid". Melanie got into the truck and we headed on our way. When she started to talk, I started to take notes. Melanie told me that working as a stripper was her 3rd job. She also helped her mother run a company and she owned her own company. When her father passed away, he left her a large trust fund and the company that makes so much money it pays for her 6 mortgages. She also thanked me for driving her. She said she owns 3 vehicles but doesn't have a driver's license in the US, only in Europe. I gathered that some of the properties she "owns" are in Europe after asking a few probing questions.

I asked her if she made good money at the club. She told me that she usually makes anywhere between $1,000 and $6,000 a night. Then she said she made $450 that night in only 3 hours. However, the amount quickly changed to $4,500 in three hours. Melanie then told me she was a widow which made me feel bad. Her husband was in the military was killed in action 2 months prior. She was now the mother of 4 children, 2 were her own and the other 2 were her husbands who she adopted when her husband's first wife passed away. At this point, I started to doubt every part of the story.

However, the story continued. I also gathered that one of the children from her husband was about to have a birthday; he was turning 12. She said she needed the extra money, so she decided to work this evening to ensure she had enough to buy airline tickets for two of her son's friends who were flying in for the birthday party. She wants to ensure the 12-year old has a fantastic birthday because she has not told him and his sibling that their father passed away 2 months ago. Question: Are you (the reader) buying any of this story?

Luckily, a gentleman at the club "bought her" for the evening. I asked what exactly that meant? She said he paid her $8000 to just sit with him, but no touching. Melanie said she is a "mean stripper". While other girls will let you hold their hand, put your arm around them, or kiss them, Melanie didn't want any men touching her. I then asked, "So what did you do to earn the $8000?" She told me she just sat with him while she worked on her lesson plans for the next day because she home schools her children.

So, let's review, Melanie made somewhere between $450 and $8000 in a short 3-hour time block. The amount kept changing so I am not exactly sure which one is correct. She has 3 vehicles, 6 properties, no license, 4 kids, 2 of the kids don't know their father is dead, a degree from Harvard (forgot to mention that one), owns a company, is a trust fund baby, who home-schools her children when she is not working at the strip club.

I don't know about you, but I think Melanie was a compulsive liar. Either that or she is the richest, most bizarre yet complicated, completely average stripper in the United States of America. All this considered, I am going to put in my application to "Chunkendales" if I can have a nightly earning potential of $8K. I'm a bit too fluffy at this point in my life to work at Chippendales.

5

THREE GUYS, TWO GIRLS, AND NO STRIP CLUB

Have you ever been in a situation that just seemed to be backward or wrong in some sense? This is what happened to me when I was dispatched to pick up William at 3 am on a Sunday morning. I drove up to a gravel parking lot at a dive bar to find 3 men and 2 women standing there waiting for me.

When I pulled up, William opened the door and was attempting to get into the front seat when one of the girls grabbed him, pulled him out of the truck and then climbed into the passenger seat on her knees with her hands on the center consul. Her face was inches from my face. I didn't get her name, but I will not soon forget her. She looked into my eyes and said, "Where can we go so I can get some boobs in my face? I want to go to a strip club now!" I looked at her and said, "do you always start your conversations this way?"

The short version of this story: the two girls wanted to go to a strip club to get lap dances, the three guys wanted to go back to their place. I would assume they didn't want to go to the strip club because it would get in the way of their agenda, but I could be incorrect. Unfortunately, all the strip clubs in the area stop sending the girls out to dance at 3 am. The two girls in the group were very sad when I told them of this tragic news. As we drove down the street, one of the girls spent most of the time on the phone with one of her female friends, threatening to come over and cuddle the girl while she was sleeping. I could tell the girl on the other end of the phone was not amused or interested.

As we got closer to the destination, the two girls wanted me to turn up the radio and then they proceeded to sing, scream, bounce around, and make complete asses out of themselves in the backseat. Of course, they told me I was an awesome driver but I'm sure that was the alcohol talking.

When we arrived, the 3 guys got out of the truck immediately. One of the girls put her arms around my neck from the backseat and thanked me for the ride. Then she whispered, "I rode all the way over here on that guy's lap and he didn't try to feel me up. I think there is something wrong with him". I responded, "evidently he's an idiot, but hopefully you will have a great morning". I was thinking to myself, *just get out already.*

As I drove off, I could see the girls walking down the middle of the street in the opposite direction, each of them holding hands with their own guy. The third guy had vanished. I can assure you this was one of the most confusing endings to a rather bizarre ride that I have encountered so far.

6

COLTON, THE BACKSEAT SINGER

Colton was one of my most favorite passengers. I had just left the Nashville airport after dropping off another rider, when I got a call 18 miles away at 5:00 AM. It took me 24 minutes to get to the Hampton Inn. I found Colton waiting outside with a duffle bag in one hand and a handful of paper in the other. He got in the back of the truck and I said, "Good Morning". The time was about 5:25 am. We were headed to Nashville. His destination was Music City Center. Music City Center is a convention center in the middle of the city. The building is massive and can easily be seen by any plane on final approach into the Nashville airport. It has been open for over 6 years and Colton was looking forward to getting there bright an early.

We had just entered the on-ramp for I-65 North when Colton says, "Would you mind if I sing to you?" This seemed like an odd request at 5:25 am.

"Um, sure" I replied, a bit confused for that time of the day. I remember thinking to myself, "perhaps I can get breakfast too out of this deal?" I told Colton I would love to hear him sing, but I warned him that I used to do some vocal coaching with barbershop quartets, choruses, and small vocal groups. This fact is true.

So, Colton began serenading me from the backseat at 5:30 in the morning. I will tell you; he did not sing softly. He belted out a song with genuine soul and charisma. So, there we were at 5:30 am, driving 70 MPH down the highway while Colton is singing at the top of his lungs in the backseat of my truck. Mind you, I was still thinking about breakfast.

I thought he sang it very well for being the first man to ever sing to me in my truck. When he was finished with his tune, I first asked him why he was singing to me. He told me that he was going to the Nashville auditions a popular TV show on NBC. I then asked him if he wanted some advice. He was very receptive of the fact that I pointed out that he was not finishing the phrases of the music. I taught him about "diphthongs" which is a musical term most of the time; sometimes it's a word I use to describe other passengers.

Anyway, we worked on the phrasing of his song and his tendency to not finish his words completely. We also talked about his confidence. We finally arrived and Colton got out of the truck, ready to conquer the world. He never expected he would have a voice lesson on his way to his audition. I don't know how he did that day, but I admit I watched the show in hopes of seeing him again. I am sure he will go far with his talent.

7

THE CROWD WITH NO SPATIAL AWARENESS

The next 16 chapters all share one thing in common, and that is the Nashville International Airport. When doing rideshare, sometimes the driver will get a request and must accept the request. Sometimes, however, the rideshare company puts the next passenger into the driver's queue so as soon as they drop off their current passenger, they are on their way to get their next passenger. This happened when I was listening to Fred counting the speed bumps during our final minutes together. I was dispatched back to Nashville to pick up Sarah. I was 20 minutes away from Sarah's location but at least I was headed in the right direction. There is nothing more frustrating than when being dispatched further and further away from home.

20 minutes later I arrived at the location where Sarah was supposed to be. I was a bit confused when I arrived because the location wasn't clearly marked. I had an address but couldn't tell if the address was the two white buildings to my right or if it was a house just beyond the two white buildings. These buildings

were rather small; my guess is each building contained 4 to 6 apartments. As I was unsure where exactly I was going, I decided to back up into the driveway between the two white buildings, so I was out of the road in case another car came down the street. I had barely put the car into park when a small crowd appeared behind the Escape. If you don't know, the Ford Escape is a very small SUV. I have seen golf carts with more room in it than my wife's SUV but as my truck was in the shop, I drove her car that morning.

I got out of the Escape to find 5 adults with large suitcases attempting to open the back hatch. I looked at them and instantly thought to myself, *these knuckleheads have absolutely no spatial awareness.*

"Um, you are not all going to fit in this vehicle," I said as I stood there looking at this group. They looked at each other with this dumbfounded look on their face. I tried my best not to be sarcastic, but I told them my vehicle didn't have the space to fit 5 people and 5 suitcases. The odd man out was a short bald fellow who looked like Uncle Fester from the Adams' Family. He got upset and said he would call another ride. He said this as he turned and walked face first into a garage door. Splat. It was hard not to laugh.

The other four piled their suitcases into the back of the SUV and they managed to squeeze themselves into the Escape. I did move my seat up as much as I could, but while the front seat passenger was comfortable, the three people in the back looked like Sardines without oil, water, or light mustard.

I could tell from the rideshare app that the group was headed to the airport. I first apologized that all of them couldn't fit in the vehicle. The passenger in front said, "that's ok, we don't like that guy anyway". I bet they were great friends. I asked them what time their flight was scheduled. and I was told 6:25 am. Mind you, we were 20 minutes away from the airport, 5:30 am, racing to make their flight without the bald guy. I suspect he did not make his flight. I'm guessing I broke a few speed limits that day, but I got the group to the airport safely. They got out, leaving no Sardine smell, and went on their way. I had another $15 in my account. I don't remember if they tipped me or not. Hopefully, they spend some money on a simple physics class or two.

8

MS. SLIPPERS

I received a call to pick up Zoe and her friend who were both heading to the airport. Zoe was nice and spent the next 10 minutes telling me about herself and the vacation she had planned. It sounded like she was going to have a lot of fun. The ride was rather uneventful until we got to the airport departure line. The drop-off area at the airport is almost always mass hysteria in the morning. It reminds me of people pushing and shoving their way to the front of the line at Disney World only they are using automobiles. Everyone thinks they have the right of way and therefore patience on the part of the rideshare driver and passenger comes in handy.

As we were waiting to park, Ms. Slippers double parked her car and began unloading. She was wearing hair curlers, butt ugly pajamas, and big fuzzy slippers. I said out loud like a drill sergeant, "Come on slippers, let's go, let's go." This made Zoe laugh. Then for some odd reason, we started chanting, "Go Slippers go, go slippers go slippers go". Zoe and her friend were grooving and dancing as I made a bit of an ass out of myself, which isn't hard to do. We all cheered on Slippers as she got back into her SUV and pulled away, leaving room for me to pull up to the curb so Zoe could exit the vehicle safely. She looked at me and said, "You're my new favorite person". This comment came with a $10 tip which Zoe added to her ride shortly after I left the airport. I still wonder to this day if Slippers was just a family member dropping off someone at the airport or, was she a rideshare driver who needs to make better apparel choices for work? Go Slippers Go.

9
KERRIE

Kerrie was another favorite passenger of mine. I thought she was very sweet although drunk and bewildered. I got a dispatch to pick up a passenger downtown Nashville. I went to the address on my mapping software and hit ARRIVE on the phone app. As I was tapping the screen, I got a phone call from the passenger who said she was around the other side of the building. I drove around and ended up spotting her on her phone exiting her hotel. Kerrie got into my truck and I looked at the app to find we were going to the airport.

Kerrie didn't have a suitcase which I found to be a bit odd. I asked her about her flight time, and she told me she had 55 minutes before boarding. I told her we were only 10 minutes away from the airport (at that time of the morning) so we should be ok. This is when she told me her clothes were at a different location. I will tell you that I have learned that sometimes you just don't ask for the rest of the story. We sped off to an air BnB on the west side of the city. Kerrie told me she would get her bag and then call another rideshare. I told her to add the location as a stop and then put the airport on the trip because she would never make it in time if I dropped her off and she requested another ride.

We arrived at her Air BnB in 6 minutes flat. 49 minutes until boarding. Kerrie jumped out and headed in to get her luggage. I took a minute to have a piece of Bubblemint gum. I love that stuff. Have you tried Bubblemint gum?

10 minutes later she returned. 39 minutes until boarding. Again, she was very sweet but had absolutely no concept of time. We got back into the truck and off we went to the airport. I arrived at BNA (Berry Field - Nashville Airport) in 11 minutes. Again, I may have broken a speed limit or two to get her there.

28 minutes until boarding. I got out and took Kerrie's suitcase out of the back of the truck. She said thanks, gave me a hug and walked casually over to the outside check-in for Southwest. I don't know if she made her flight, but she was the first passenger to ever give me a hug for doing my best to get her to the airport as fast as possible.

10

JERSEY MIKE'S

If you want a great sandwich, I highly suggest *Jersey Mike's*. When I first moved to Nashville, I discovered their buffalo chicken ranch jumbo sandwich with bacon, and I have been a fan ever since. So, you can imagine that it made me smile when I was called to *Jersey Mikes* in north Nashville to pick up Sean. I figured he was getting off work and I was going to take him home. That story made sense in my head. The real story to this day still does not make sense.

When I arrived at *Jersey Mike's*, I found Sean at the curb with a suitcase. When I find a passenger with a suitcase, it usually means I am heading to the airport to drop them off. After I hit ARRIVE on the app, I looked at the location and sure enough, I was heading to the airport. I got out of the truck and loaded the suitcase into the back as I always do for passengers heading to the airport. Sean got into the front seat. I immediately asked him if he had a buffalo chicken sandwich before he called me? He did not. He told me he was just parking his car in the parking lot while he was away.

Now, as he is telling me this story, I was slowly making my way through the parking lot where I politely pointed out the BIG sign that said, "No overnight parking, violators will be towed at owner's expense". I asked Sean if he was sure he wanted to leave his car? After all, he was taking a rideshare to the airport; he had options. I could have picked him up at his house where his car would be safe and sound, or he could park in long-term parking for $11 a day. Sean told me he was only going to be gone for 3 days and he would rather take his chances. I'm thinking to myself, $33 for parking or $350 for towing. It's not a hard decision to make unless your name is Sean.

I arrived at the airport and Sean went on his way. I don't know if he was towed or if his gamble paid off. He was hoping the sign was just a deterrent and that no one would really tow his vehicle before he came back from his trip. I kept my fingers crossed for him because he seemed like a nice guy.

11

THE CAR SEAT
INCIDENT

Some passengers are funny, and they make me laugh. Some rides, however, make me very angry and this passenger was no exception. This was another passenger named Scott. I was on my way to pick him up when he called and told me I was going to pick up his girlfriend and her young daughter. I asked how old the daughter was and Scott told me she was 7. I asked if his girlfriend had a car seat because children that small should be in a car seat. After all, it's a law in every state. Scott blew off the request and hung up. I arrived at the girlfriend's house and she came out with her small daughter. The girlfriend was very nice and so was the daughter. They, of course, were running late for their flight. They were heading to the airport.

As a rideshare driver, passengers constantly put us in an awkward position. The child could have been tall enough where she didn't need a car seat, but as the driver, I shouldn't have to be put into that position. It's better to be safe than sorry. I should have demanded the car seat or canceled the ride. I admit I may have made the wrong decision by letting the girl ride in the back, although she did wear her seatbelt. Her mom sat next to her with her own seatbelt tightly fastened, holding her daughter. I drove slowly because I felt very uncomfortable.

Share My Ride

I would suggest to all parents that simply because you take a LYFT, UBER, or TAXI, the laws in your state don't change. If your child rides in a car seat in your car, they need to ride in a car seat in the rideshare vehicle as well. Scott seemed to have little regard for the child's safety as I could tell by his answer and behavior on the phone. Little does he know that I rated him a 1 star out of 5 stars. Had I canceled the ride the girlfriend would have probably missed her flight. This is the dilemma that rideshare drivers sometimes face. Passengers don't realize the law doesn't cease to exist in a rideshare vehicle or taxi.

12

THE LADY WITH
THE BANDAGE
ON HER FACE

Every now and then, I will get a request to go pick up a passenger and LYFT will send a message that says, "this is the passenger's first-time using LYFT". Anytime I pick up someone who has never used the service before, I feel it's my responsibility to make a good first impression. When I got to Cindy's house in North Nashville, I did just that. I pulled into an extremely long driveway and drove to the top, did a three-point turn and put the truck into park. I had arrived. As short time later Cindy appeared with a suitcase, packed and ready to head to the airport.

As Cindy said, "Hello" I noticed a very large Band-Aid on her forehead. This was not an average size bandage, but rather one of those large ones that are 5 to 6 inches across. When she got into the truck, I asked her if this was, in fact, her first ride? It was and so I welcomed her, and we headed down the long driveway on our way to the airport which was approximately 20 miles away. I had to ask about the bandage because something that large can't be hidden. Cindy told me she had a "bit of a fender bender" the day before. In fact, she crashed her car which was probably why I was driving her to the airport. During the crash, she smacked her head on the steering wheel as she slammed into a driver in front of her. I immediately wondered if she had a concussion and challenged if she should even be going on a trip after such a traumatic event? Cindy assured me she was ok and had plenty of Tylenol in case the pain started to get to her.

When someone tells you that they drove into the back of another car, what comes to mind? I first think of someone texting, or perhaps the driver in front stops suddenly. Accidents can occur from issues such as tailgating, fatigue, speeding, or intoxication. When I asked Cindy, she turned a bit red and freely admitted she was eating oatmeal. Wait, what? I think I blinked a few times before saying, "say again?" Yep, Cindy was eating oatmeal with a spoon while driving on a busy road, on a wet day in traffic.

She was very sweet, but not the brightest bulb in the box (which she admitted). After a good laugh, we made our way to the airport. I swear you can't make this stuff up.

Note to self: never eat a bowl of oatmeal in bumper to bumper traffic.

13

MR. MONEYBAGS

Some of the experiences I have doing rideshare do not involve passengers. One day I was sitting in the airport queue at Nashville International airport. This queue is a geo-fenced area for LYFT and UBER drivers, operating on the "first in, first out" rule. To put it simply, any rideshare driver can show up at the airport and enter the rideshare waiting area. The area tracks who was in the lot first and they go to the top of the list. When a passenger at the airport requests a ride, the person at the top of the list gets the request. The app will tell a driver by way of a small message at the top of the screen, "there are 5 drivers ahead of you" or "there are 76 drivers ahead of you". If you think the "76" was a joke, you have never seen the rideshare queue at the airport on a Friday or Saturday night.

During the waiting period, drivers have time to waste. Most of them take a nap or read the paper. Some get out of their vehicles and talk to each other, take a smoke break, or use the Porto-Potti which is provided by the airport. This is also a time for driver posturing. Every rideshare driver seems to think they have secrets that others do not. They all "know the system" better than anyone else. Every driver wants other drivers to believe he (or she) makes more money than anyone else. I will admit, I sat in the queue one time and found that most of the posturing drivers are completely full of crap.

A young driver parked next to me as I sat there waiting for my turn at the front of the line. He drove a beat-up Toyota Prius. When he got out to smoke, he walked to my truck window which was down at the time so I could get some fresh air. Immediately, he asked me about how much gas my truck uses? Again, here comes more posturing from a Zen master of rideshare. He then proceeded to tell me that I would never make any money in a truck and that the real money could only be made if I owned a Toyota Prius. He then told me he gets very upset when he doesn't make at a minimum $400 a day doing rideshare.

I began to run some simple napkin math in my head. If Mr. Moneybags was pulling in $400 a day, working 5 days a week, (accounting for 2 weeks of unpaid vacation each year), he would be making about $100,000 a year doing UBER before taxes, gas, depreciation, etc. That's a heck of a salary from a guy who went to take a smoke break, got in his car, and slept for an hour before I got a ride request and left the parking lot. I have to hand it to him. It's not easy making $100K while taking an hour here and there for a nap. His big mistake was really with thinking my truck would be my downfall. Little did Zen boy know that I hear many stories from passengers who request a ride and when a driver with a Toyota Prius shows up to find 3 or 4 people heading to the airport with large suitcases, the Prius can't handle the load. The passenger must cancel and request someone else with a larger vehicle. I also get many compliments and tips because the F-150 is spacious and clean.

Hopefully, Mr. Moneybags is securing his fortune, be it in cash, cigarettes, or time spent in nappy time.

14

SERVICE ANIMALS

Rideshare drivers must accept service animals in their vehicle, without exception. Both UBER and LYFT can deactivate a driver if they refuse to accept a service animal in their vehicle. Given that I love dogs and most pets, I was looking forward to the first time I had a service animal climb on board the F-150. Finally, I met Mr. Bentley. Mr. Bentley was a small, ugly Shih Tzu who was very friendly and about to take his first flight. The little pup hopped up into the F-150 and when his mom got settled in, we started thru the condo parking lot towards the airport. 30 seconds later his mom realized she forgot her wallet, so we did a quick turn around and went back to the apartment. While she went back into her apartment to find her wallet, Mr. Bentley and I got better acquainted. Mr. Bentley was cute yet ugly. He had bad breath, but he was a very excited puppy. After all, this would be his first airplane ride and he was riding up top rather than in a kennel in the luggage department.

When his mother returned, she was tickled pink that her puppy was up front in my lap because evidently, Mr. Bentley doesn't like most men. But who couldn't love this face? I know you can't see me, but I'm pretty cute, just like Mr. Bentley.

10 minutes later I arrived at the airport and I said "Goodbye" to Mr. Bentley. He strutted into the airport like any happy puppy would if they were going on a big adventure.

15
MUSHROOMS
IN DENVER

Occasionally I will get comments in the F-150 about drugs. These conversations could be about prescription drugs or the use of pot in Nashville. Often riders will get into the truck and say, "At least your car doesn't smell like weed". My response is usually, "Do you always start conversations this way?" I think it's sad that so many rideshare drivers think it's ok to smoke pot while driving, but that is another topic for another day.

I picked up William at his condo on the west side of Nashville. I could tell when he opened her door with a giant suitcase that he was heading to the airport. Once I confirmed my arrival on the app, which I sometimes forget to do right away, I could see I was going to take him to the airport and drop him off at the Southwest door. I got out, greeted him, took his suitcase and loaded it into the back of the truck, and then we were ready to go.

On the way, I asked him where he was heading, and he replied that he was going to Denver to go skiing with his friends for the weekend. There is nothing quite like a long weekend skiing in Denver, so I am told. We chit chatted for a few minutes and then he received a phone call. The phone call was from a friend who was about to leave for the airport. The friend was calling William to ask him what kind of container he should use for the "mushrooms" so they would get through security. I have to stop and think, "what kind of idiot would knowingly attempt to take illegal drugs on an airplane" but alas there are thousands of them out there in the world.

William advised him that he should probably leave them at home because they could get more in Denver when they arrived. In May 2019, Denver voted to decriminalize the use of Mushrooms so buying them when the group got to town was a much better plan than attempting to smuggle them through airport security.

It's a good thing to have a game plan when heading out for a long weekend. Sometimes, the plan includes leaving the drugs at home and appropriating more when you get to your destination. I will have to remember that the next time I am packing my extra strength Excedrin in my suitcase.

16
DENNIS AND MR. KEMPNER

Sometimes when I am driving at night, things happen that are not funny, sad, or eventful. Sometimes, situations are simply ironic. Early morning on a Tuesday while my wife was out of town, I decided to drive from 11 pm to 5 am. The reason I did this is so I would be home by 6 am to feed the animals breakfast since I am a responsible pet owner. I picked up a guy around 1 am at the airport who needed a ride home. His name was Dennis and he just landed in Nashville on his way home from spring break. When I asked him about his trip, he told me he was in Cuba for a week which I thought was a rather odd place to spend spring break but to each their own. I dropped him off and he headed into his condo very tired from his trip.

Later that morning, around 3 am I picked up Mr. Kempner who requested a ride to the airport. When I arrived, he was waiting with two very large suitcases, a musical instrument which I think was a trombone, and a briefcase. I loaded the luggage into the truck and off we went. I asked him where he was heading, and he told me he was going to Cuba? He works with a missionary group and is the leader of their band. The band is a small brass ensemble. One of the suitcases was filled with toothbrushes, toothpaste, and other items that are hard to get in Cuba.

I mention this because Cuba is one of those locations that is not in high demand and I thought it was rather strange to pick up someone coming from Cuba and then drop off someone going to Cuba on the same night. I have completed over 1000 rideshare rides and that night was the first and last time any passenger ever included Cuba in their travel plans.

17

WATCH OUT FOR ROCKS?

Now, let's talk about some crazy police stories! When driving in the early morning, I see things that make me want to scratch my head and wonder, "what on earth is going on and what planet am I on?" Traffic laws in Nashville seem to be optional in the morning. Red lights don't seem to stop the average motorist in the morning. Occasionally I will see blue flashing lights, indicating the boys in blue are doing their job. I think the police in this town have a tough job, and on this occasion, I was very happy to see them.

I was dispatched to pick up Mike who was going to the airport. He was a scruffy character who was on his way home after a weekend of partying with his friends. If memory serves, he was heading home to Denver, Colorado. I headed to the airport and Mike told me about his weekend which included partying on Broadway which is what everyone seems to do when they vacation in Nashville. The time was around 4:30 am and traffic was almost non-existent. We were taking the back way into the airport on a road called Harding Place. My car was the only car on the road until I looked ahead and saw a police officer pull out into our lane, perpendicular to the road, stop, and then put his flashing blue lights on for all to see. He was blocking our lane. The officer was about 150 yards ahead of us.

I slowed down, put on my turn signal and pulled into the right lane. At that very moment, another police officer pulled into my lane, again, blocking the road with his lights on.

So, let's recap. I was 100 yards away from two police officers with their lights on, who were now blocking both lanes of Harding Place. I pulled up slowly as Mike and I wondered what on earth was going on with these two cops? I rolled down the passenger window as I pulled up to the cop car. I asked if I could pass by since Mike and I were on our way to the airport? The cop replied, "yes, just go slow and watch out for the rocks."

I looked at Mike and said, "what the hell is he talking about?" As I pulled into the passing lane at a brisk 5 miles an hour, Mike and I passed the two cop cars and saw the rocks. From our vantage point, it looked like a dump truck full of gravel had dropped its entire load in the middle of Harding Place. Was this an accident or a disgruntled employee who took a dump with his truck? I remind you (the reader) this is an extremely busy road during the day. The speed limit is 35 and if Mike and I had hit that pile of gravel at 4:30 am in the pitch dark, it would have most likely totaled my truck. The gravel was the size of my fist, so I'm talking about some good size rocks in the middle of the road. The pile was so large that special equipment had to be brought in to clean up the mess.

I dropped Mike off at the airport and I was dispatched to another call. The GPS directed me back down Harding Place. I was now on the other side of the road. There was a very long line of traffic slowly making their way, one car at a time around the two police officers who were still guarding their pile of rocks. I figure they were enjoying a donut as images of Monty Python and the Holy Grail went thru my head, *None shall pass!*

18

THE TRUCK
ACCIDENT

One day I was out driving for 7 hours, having a pretty good day I would add, so I decided it was time to head home. I was hungry and my bladder was not at all happy with me. I set the filter on my rideshare app to find me rides that would get me closer to home, but alas there were no rides to be found. When I am looking for a ride I tend to drive slower. There is nothing more annoying than getting a ride request 10 seconds after you speed past the street or exit where you should have turned. So, I headed for home in no hurry.

I was traveling down I-24 towards exit 66a which is my exit. I was following a tractor in search of a trailer, owned by some cold-haul company. I was keeping a safe distance when we both got off the highway at exit 66a which was under some construction, though the exit was still open. All of a sudden, the tractor came to an abrupt halt immediately upon entering the exit ramp. This was a shock, but I slammed on my brakes and I came to a complete stop as well. I was about 30 feet behind the tractor, wondering *what on earth* was going on because I couldn't see any construction equipment in the way. I sat there for a second and then I beeped my horn. Perhaps the driver could see something happening that I couldn't see given our positions on the ramp. Then disaster struck.

For some strange reason, the driver had determined the exit was closed and that a better strategy would be to put his tractor in reverse, back out on to the highway, and continue to another exit. Clearly, the driver was a complete knucklehead. He put the tractor in reverse and before I could react, he slammed into the front of my truck as I laid on the horn, desperately trying to put my truck into reverse in the blink of an eye. After the impact, I seem to remember swearing very loudly in my truck, after all my F-150 was completely paid for and had not a scratch on it at the time.

The bewildered knucklehead got out of his truck and walked back to me. He said that he didn't see my bright orange/red truck behind him. I asked him if he looked in the mirror, they usually work pretty well. He said he did but I know he didn't. I asked him, "why on earth he would back up on an off-ramp?" He said, "I thought the exit was closed". I replied to the 23-year old knucklehead, "If the ramp was closed, there would be great big signs that say, 'RAMP CLOSED'." I immediately began taking pictures of everything to include his license, truck, my truck, etc. We called the police to get a police report. I would encourage anyone who ever gets into an accident with a commercial vehicle to always get a police report. Some companies will try anything and everything to get out of paying an accident claim if you do not have a police report.

It took 25 minutes for the police to show up. Obviously, an accident on an offramp is a very low priority for the boys in blue. The officer walked up to me and asked me what had happened. I would guess that most of the time when a truck has damage in the front it's due to running into the vehicle in front of it. The officer gave me a very confused look when I told him that the tractor had backed into me on the off ramp. As I finished telling him what happened, the knucklehead walked up and the officer looked at him and said, "what happened?" "I thought the ramp was closed and then I backed into his truck," said the astute young driver. The officer laughed and looked at me with the reaffirming look that told me this idiot just admitted his guilt and all would be fine. The officer asked both of us for proper documentation and went back to his car to begin filling out the necessary paperwork.

I should tell you that I did find some humor in this whole story as there was another officer in the car who came out with his cohort, stood there with the stereotypical mirrored sunglasses, but he never said a word. He just stood there like a goofball in an attempt to look threatening. After handing my documentation to the officer in charge, the second officer who I shall refer to as "Gumby", got back into the car, took his hat off, and promptly went to sleep against the window while the first officer did his paperwork. He was basically useless in this situation.

5 or 10 minutes later, I looked in my rearview mirror to see Gumby wake up, get out of the vehicle, put on his hat, and walk toward my truck. I had no idea what he wanted, but I put my window down. "I took a look and your vehicle is not

leaking any fluids, just thought I would let you know" replied Gumby. Then he turned around and went back to the police car. He took off his hat, got inside, and went back to sleep against the passenger window. I am very thankful that he took the time out of his nap to make that brief report. Great work Gumby!

To end this story, I will tell you that my truck ultimately had $4800 in damage to the front end. My insurance handled everything promptly and got me a rental within 2 hours. This is key information because a rideshare driver may not use a rental car to drive LYFT or UBER unless the driver is renting the vehicle from LYFT or UBER. Therefore, while my truck was in the shop, I was driving my wife's Ford Escape. Now you know why some of these stories refer to my truck while others refer to her miniature SUV. With that being said, I sleep better at night knowing Gumby is on the job.

19

TWO YOUNG LADIES AND A POLICE CHASE

The title of this short story is as crazy as it sounds. I woke up on a Saturday morning and headed out around 2:45 am. I began heading towards Nashville and once I was on the highway, my app started flashing at me. I was heading to pick up Kelli. The GPS told me I needed to get off the next exit. I drove down the exit ramp where I needed to turn left to go under the highway overpass on my way to the destination.

When I turned, I noticed a car coming down the exit ramp from the opposite direction at an incredibly high rate of speed. The car whipped around the corner and sped off in the same direction I was heading, the car fishtailing as it went around that corner. I said, "Holy Crap" out loud as I saw this happen. I am not sure I have ever seen a car turn a corner so fast. The driver nearly lost control. Then I saw flashing blue lights, the police were hot on the tail of the first car. The police took the corner fast as well, trying to hit the back corner of the first vehicle to spin it out and bring it to a stop. I have watched enough TV to know what the police were attempting to do, but they missed. The car then took another corner and sped down a very wide road like a bullet shot out of a gun. It was quite the wakeup call to watch all this up close.

I then proceeded to pick up Kelli at a small restaurant. She got into the truck with her friend. Both girls were dressed like hookers with dresses that weren't even long enough to cover their panties. When they walked to the truck, they spent most of the time pulling down their dresses which probably fit them 15 years prior. They were both very nice and said hello when they got into the backseat. I did notice that Kelli's friend had a lower voice than mine, but I left it at that.

Off we headed to their destination which took me back to the same exit where the cop was chasing the car. When we approached the exit, now traveling in the opposite direction, here came another police car. He was also traveling at a very high rate of speed, lights flashing as he headed down the same road where I saw the first police car disappear. As I got on the highway, here comes another police car, lights flashing. 15 seconds later, another police car followed by another police car, both with lights flashing. All of them took the same exit so my guess is the person they were chasing was in some serious trouble.

Three miles up the road I saw 3 more cops on the other side of the highway that had boxed in another vehicle. I don't know if this was related to the incident I just described, but I could tell they were not there to change a flat tire. Whoever was in that vehicle that was boxed in was about to be in handcuffs. Again, I watch too much TV. I won't ever know because I scoured the internet the next day to find out what happened, but I came up empty.

When I arrived at the destination with Kelli, it was a rather questionable hotel. Both ladies got out and then asked me if I wanted to join them? I politely declined, and into the hotel they disappeared. I remember thinking to myself, *at 49-years old and a bit fluffy, at least I'm not losing my sex appeal.* I got another request as they were getting out of the truck, so I was quickly off to my next ride. I never know how my day is going to begin, but this one definitely awakened me.

On a side note, I saw 3 major car crashes on that morning. I counted a total of 18 cops that day with their lights flashing. I ended my day early because, with all the crazy drivers and police activity, I took the high road and went home to have pancakes. Sometimes it's not worth being out on the roads when there is an overabundance of police activity.

20
EZEKIAL - ARRESTED FOR DUI

Some drivers get nervous when they deal with the police. Imagine my surprise when I was dispatched to the police station. I didn't know what to expect but headed that way just the same. When I pulled up to the destination, an officer in uniform was standing at the sidewalk where the small icon on my app told me to go. I thought to myself that perhaps the officer needed a ride home? I pulled up to him and he looked at me with this look that said, "get out of my way you jackass". It turns out, he wasn't the passenger who needed a ride. The officer walked around the truck after I stopped and headed across the street, through a secret door to what I guessed would be the police motor pool or the super-secret donut shop.

Shortly after the officer disappeared thru the super-secret door, Ezekial jumped into the front seat of the truck. He was not having a good night. He told me that he had been arrested for drunk driving. Then he told me his car and his wife had been impounded. No, I am not making this up. He told me his wife had been impounded. I didn't know that was a thing.

I asked Ezekial where he was pulled over, but he didn't know. I asked him what time he was pulled over, he didn't know. I was starting to wonder if he was actually sober. I gathered that he was drinking heavily and was pulled over driving a silver PT Cruiser. I think he should have been arrested just for driving the PT Cruiser, but I digress. I also question why the police wouldn't tell him where his wife was when he was released from custody? I am sure there is more to that story.

I drove Ezekial back to his friend's house. He was just visiting Nashville for a few days of R&R. I did mention that I knew about the impound lot and that he would most likely have to pay nearly $400 to get his car back. I don't think he was amused at my attempt to share nuggets of knowledge I have learned from other astute ride share riders.

21
THE CANADIANS

Nashville is a party town. Many people come to this city each week to listen to live music and drink. This city is a top destination for bachelorette parties which can be found in every honkytonk on Broadway street on any Friday or Saturday night. This is also a popular destination for people from other countries which is currently evident as the airport is expanding by building an international terminal. Therefore, it was no surprise when I got a call from a group of Canadians who had just arrived in town.

I got a call from Joe and his friends around 11 pm on a Friday night. When I got to the destination, I found an apartment complex that was surrounded by a security fence. A security code was needed to get into the complex. Another car was at the gate when I arrived, and my plan was to zip thru the gate when it opened for the first car. I sat there and sat there and sat there. The first car was an UBER driver who didn't speak much English. I could tell because I could hear him on the phone as his passenger was telling him how to punch the security code into the gate. I had sat there for several minutes watching this idiot try to get into the gate. I finally called Joe to tell him I was there, but I was waiting behind this UBER driver. Joe told me the gate code which I shouted out to the idiot UBER driver. The code was 3899# but the UBER driver kept punching in #3899. Finally, he figured it out and I did what I had planned on doing, I zipped thru the gate while it was still open for "Zippy the wonder driver" in front of me.

It turns out, the UBER driver was there to pick up half of Joe's group and I was there to pick up the other half. When Joe got into the front seat, I apologized that it took so long to get him and that he made the right choice getting into my truck rather than Zippy's vehicle. We headed for downtown. I asked Joe where he was from and all of his friends in the backseat told me they were from Canada. They drove 12 hours from Toronto, a total of 770 miles. Of course, the first thing you want to do after driving from Canada to Nashville is to get into another vehicle and go drinking. Personally, I would have gone to bed but that's just me. Joe and his friends planned on being out all night, drinking their way from bar to bar to bar to bar.

I followed Zippy who was obviously ahead of me and we both arrived at Honkytonk Central where Joe and his friends got out and began their bar hop. I hope they had a great time. I was tired just thinking about it.

22
RICK

I picked up Rick from a hotel and took him to the airport. Rick was a nice guy who was here in town on business. There was nothing interesting about this ride other than it was raining. We were about halfway to the airport when I turned up the radio. John Denver was singing, "Leaving on a Jet Plane". I said nothing but I did laugh. The next song, (I'm not making this up) was Neil Sedaka singing "Laughter in the rain".

Irony?

23
LINCOLN THE SINGER

I picked up Lincoln one morning and headed to the airport. Lincoln happens to be the lead singer of a band that I had to research on the internet when I got home. For privacy sake, I will keep the name of the bad out of this story. They're a great band with really "hip" music. Anyway, the ride with Lincoln was just another ride to the airport but it's what we saw on our way that captured our attention. The weather was not cooperating with us and so it was raining very hard. There is a spot on the highway heading east toward the airport that collects the water and is dangerous if you don't know how to drive or if you hit that spot too fast. Sure enough, someone did just that. They hit the water that had collected on the road so hard that they spun their SUV and managed to launch it such that it landed on the metal barricade on the side of the road. I don't really understand how the driver managed to balance the car as they did. It was fascinating although it was slowing down traffic. This is not good when someone has a plane to catch.

I drove Lincoln to the airport and he went on his way.

I ended up passing the scene of the accident about an hour later and while the SUV was gone, the damage remained. Three police cars were blocking the road because the metal barricade was now out in the middle of the lane. I would guess the tow truck did that damage when it pulled the SUV down off its perch. Another 45 minutes later I was heading back to the airport for the 6th time that morning and the barricade was pushed off to the side of the road and all lanes were open. I still can't figure out how that vehicle got up on that perch. Fascinating.

24

DILLAN AND HIS CELL PHONE

I was out driving at 3 am in Nashville and I received a call to pick up Dillan and his friends from a local strip club. When I arrived, they were outside ready to go which was nice as I didn't have to park and wait which is common when picking up people from a club. Dillan and his friends jumped into the vehicle rather disappointed. They went to see some girls but when they arrived, the girls were done dancing for the night. They left no sooner than they arrived. I took them back to the Air BnB that they had rented for the weekend. I dropped them off and went on to my next dispatch.

The next rider needed to go to the airport. When we arrived at the airport, the passenger opened the door to get out and a cell phone fell out of the truck, landing on the curb. The passenger asked me if it was my cell phone as I unloaded two suitcases from the back of the truck. Given that I had only driven one other passenger so far that day, I knew it had to belong to the group of guys I had dropped off on the other side of Nashville. I intended to try to swing back to their house if I was over that way, but unfortunately, the morning was very busy, and I didn't have a chance.

The phone was locked, and I didn't make any attempts at guessing a password, but I could see messages that were coming through to the home screen. One text was from a friend of Dillan who said they needed to find a stripper who could come over to the AirBnB. Great idea! Another message was from his girlfriend though I don't remember what it said. The next message was the one I was waiting for. The message said, "This phone has been lost. If found, call this number" and a phone number was listed below. I immediately called the number and got an answering machine. I tried several more times but was unsuccessful. I then sent the rideshare company a message stating that I had found a phone and believed it belonged to Dillan.

To make a long story short, after a plethora of back and forth messages I ended up meeting Dillan at a local McDonalds later that day. I had to drive 12 miles from my house to the McDonalds and another 12 home. When I arrived, Dillan came up to my window, handed me a $20 bill and I handed him his phone. I let the rideshare company know that the device had been returned and they gave me a $15 credit to my account. So, I made $15 on the ride and $35 for chasing around a cell phone all day. It was a bit of a hassle but financially worthwhile.

The sad part is, I don't know if the guys ever found their stripper????

25
THE T-SHIRT GUY

Since this city is full of drunk people, I thought I would switch to a few stories about drunk people. I grew up watching the Dukes of Hazzard. It is not exactly great TV, but it was popular enough that it has its own museum here in Nashville across the street from the Gaylord Convention Center. It's called Cooters and it's FREE. I don't think anyone in their right mind would pay to go into that place, however, I do admit that anyone who comes to visit me in Nashville is promptly hauled into Cooters. You can ask any of my friends who will assure you, I love that place.

So, I was very happy when I got a call to pick up Fred at the hotel next door to Cooters. I should mention the time was 4:30 am and the temperature outside was about 27 degrees with wind. There is nothing worse than a cold, windy morning. However, the morning gets better when you find a drunk guy in shorts, walking through the parking lot of Cooters and he is your passenger!

I stopped the car as I was driving the Ford Escape that morning, and Fred got in. I should note that the Escape has seat warmers which come in handy when you pick up a drunk guy in shorts when it's 27 degrees outside. "You are a lifesaver" he drooled as the smell of beer began to permeate the vehicle. I asked him where he was going and he said, "Hendersonville".

Hendersonville was about 19 miles north so Fred and I would be spending some time together. Fred was very nice. He spent most of the ride telling me about his job. Fred travels with concert tours all over the country selling T-shirts. Perhaps some of the people reading this book have purchased a T-shirt at a rock concert from Fred and didn't even know it. I got an earful about the world of T-shirt sales and Fred repeated himself over and over, but he was intoxicated so I don't hold this against him.

I got Fred to his destination which was an apartment complex. The thing I hate the most about apartment complexes in this town is the overabundance of speed bumps. Fred, however, knew that we needed to go over 7 of them on the way to his place. He counted them as we went over each one, two, three, four, etc. I will tell you that nothing surprises me anymore, but I was shocked when Fred asked me if he could tip me in cash and promptly handed me a $20 bill. I never knew if Fred was such a generous guy or if the alcohol impaired his ability to distinguish between a $5 and a $20. Fred was very nice and overall the ride was fun. Fred smelled, but the seat warmers in the Ford Escape helped me to get an extra $20 on top of the $15 fare.

26
ADJUSTING TO FRANK

Frank was one of my favorite passengers. I found him stumbling through a parking lot in Nashville. He climbed into the truck and said hello in an extremely loud voice. I asked Frank about his night and he said he had been out since 7 pm the night before. The time was now 5 am. That's 10 solid hours of drinking.

Frank had just returned from vacationing in Greenland. That's not exactly where I would have gone for vacation, but Frank was really jazzed about his trip. He started to tell me about it when all of the sudden we passed a high school. Frank stopped his story, looked at the high school and started to point. "That high school – has – a – really good" he belched, "4H program".

He continued, "there is nothing quite like seeing a goat giving birth. It's truly beautiful. I wish humans could give birth and be as beautiful as goats". Thanks for that epiphany Frank. I'm not sure I agree, but Frank was very passionate about watching goats giving birth.

Then, the conversation changed again when Frank looked at me and said, "Are you adjusted?" I looked at him and said, "adjusted? Yep, I'm adjusted." I had no idea where this conversation was going. Frank continued, "It's good to be adjusted, I'm just saying".

I still have no idea what Frank was talking about as we pulled up to his house. He fell out of the truck when he opened the door. He turned to grab his phone and he said goodbye. I almost wish I could have driven him around for another 30 minutes to see what other interesting nuggets of knowledge he would throw at me.

27

THE DRUNK
BARTENDER

I was driving very early morning, around 3:15 am and I received a rideshare request from Melrose. I arrived at the location about 10 minutes later and a bald, African American gentleman walked to the truck. He looked just like his picture. He opened the door and said, "She will be right out". Obviously, I would not be taking Melrose anywhere and this made me sad. 2 minutes later, a tall blonde woman comes staggering out of the house. *Oh yay*, I thought to myself, *she's bombed.*

The drunk lady was tall, blonde, and looked like she needed to eat a steak. She gave Melrose a big hug and a kiss on the lips, then another hug. Melrose opened the rear passenger door and she crawled into the F-150. "That man is my best friend" she exclaimed. "He is my best friend. That man is my best friend" so sayeth the drunk blonde in the backseat. She told me this about 9 times before I finally established that Melrose was in fact, her best friend. "But he tried to get on me and I am just not like that" she yammered. I really didn't want to hear the rest of the story, but I got it anyway. The blonde went on to talk for 30 minutes straight as I drove quietly to her home. She told me about Melvin, who was her best friend. I also learned about her boyfriend who had a 9-year crack addiction, and her father the pastor. She told me that she was a bartender who could have been anything in the world but alas at this time, she was a pastor's daughter with a crackhead boyfriend and a best friend named Melrose.

I am not sure what else she told me because I freely admit I tuned out of the conversation. "I would rather be having breakfast with Colton the singer, but I am stuck with this bimbo instead," I thought to myself. When we arrived at her place, the blonde sat up like a squirrel in the backseat, on red alert, looking for a vehicle or a canister of nuts. She never described the vehicle to me, but I assume she was searching for the vehicle owned by the crackhead boyfriend. She then spouted off about how she made really good tips and she wanted to give me a good tip. I was then handed 3 sweaty $1 bills.

I felt the need for some Clorox wipes as I thanked her, watched her stumble out of the truck, and then I drove away. I was on the lookout for the crackhead boyfriend, who could have been driving any one of the 100 cars in plain sight.

Melrose should think about getting a new friend. Oddly enough, I never knew her name. She never told me, Melrose never mentioned it, and the crackhead never showed up. My loss.

28
ANOTHER DRUNK GIRL

If you decide to do rideshare, it's inevitable that you will pick up someone who is drunk. You run the risk of them puking in your car if you drive too fast, if the temperature is too hot, or if you drive on winding roads. I usually drive in the morning because I would rather take people to the airport or to work. However, one morning when I logged into the rideshare app, the first request I received was from the hotel that is only 2 miles from my house. When I arrived, I found two girls who stumbled to the truck. Oy Vey, here I go again.

When they got into the back seat, I could tell immediately that they were sloshed. I asked them if they had been out partying all night and of course, I was correct. They were drinking on Broadway in Nashville. Broadway is where you will find all the honky-tonk bars, music, and hundreds (if not thousands) of drunk people. The girls had requested a rideshare when they were downtown. The driver drove them from downtown to my town, which was about 18 miles from their home. Evidently, one of the girls said she felt sick and so the rideshare driver pulled over and promptly kicked them out of his car. What a jerk. If you drive at night, driving drunk people is part of the job. This is the reason I don't drive at night. I felt bad for the two girls, so I took them home. It was a slow ride with the air conditioning on medium. One girl slept all the way home. The other wanted to chit chat so I obliged.

When we were 2 miles from her house, she asked me to pull over. She got out on the side of the road and spent the next 5 minutes dry-heaving, but nothing came out. I was very happy about that little nugget of knowledge that she shared as soon as she got back into the truck. I drove her home to her apartment complex. I should reiterate again that I hate speed bumps. Even if you drive over them slowly, they are no friend to the drunk person in the back seat. I will say, I got her home with clean seats in the back of my truck although she puked as soon as she got out of the truck and then stumbled into her apartment. I breathed a sigh of relief and was ready to head to my next call as it started to rain. So, there she went; drunk, tired, and wet. The Nashville trifecta.

29

TWO DRUNK GUYS IN NASHVILLE

When using the rideshare app, when a driver gets close to the destination, the app will show you if the passenger is on the right or left side of the street. This feature is very handy as many times the house numbers are not properly displayed on the mailbox. Riders are very annoyed when their driver arrives late or has trouble finding their place, even though they often do nothing to help out by putting their house number on the mailbox in a way that is visible to a passing motorist. But I digress. I was dispatched to pick up Brady in downtown Nashville at 5 am on a Sunday morning.

As I got closer to the destination, I was having trouble determining if the passenger was on the right side or left side of the road because the little yellow person icon used by the rideshare company was in the middle of the road. Sure enough, I found Brady walking down the middle of 9th avenue with his friend. I will admit, it's easy to find your rider when they are smack dab in the middle of the road. Brady and his friend crawled into the backseat of the truck. They told me they had been out on the town since 9 pm the previous night. 8 hours of solid drinking must be good for the soul. I drove them 3 blocks to their hotel. They could have stumbled there in the time it took me to get from my last drop off to their location. They were surprised as they stated in a slurred, drunken voice, "We are here already?" I proceeded to tell them the trip took over 15 minutes and they slept the whole way. Sadly, they believed me. Brady says to me, "Thanks man, I can't believe we're so wasted, you're like a life saver bro" and then he got out of the truck. Ride over. The "life saver" drove 3 whole blocks. *Sleep well boys, you had a rough night* I thought to myself as I headed on to my next adventure.

30

TWO DRUNK NERDS

Most of the time, drunk people are entertaining. There are stories about drunk people puking in the back of their rideshare vehicle, but this doesn't happen nearly as much as people may be led to believe. Another fact that I have found to be true: drunk people can be picked up at all times of the day.

At 8 am on a Saturday morning, I got a request to pick up a guy in East Nashville. When I arrived in the driveway, two guys were heading toward the truck. One of them was carrying a full case of Budweiser. I could tell this was going to be fun. They were very friendly and courteous as they got into the backseat and we pulled out of the driveway, heading for the destination.

These guys were ripped. I could tell they had been drinking all night which was confirmed when one of them told me, "we've been drinking all night". The two of them sat in the backseat and had a very sophisticated conversation using as many words from the thesaurus as they could fit into a sentence. Each of them was trying to be a sesquipedalian orator while discussing whether or not single girls were hotter when they are pregnant? Granted, this is a riveting topic among men; not!

While 'hot chicks who are pregnant' was the main topic, for a moment the subject changed over to politics. One of the orators said and I quote, "we are witnessing the 'pussification' of America." Meaning, kids these days are soft and weak thanks to participation awards and the fact that some parents fight their kid's battles for them, so kids never learn to stand up for themselves.

The second orator responded, "cool word dude". Inventing words must be a "cool" thing these days. However, soon they were back to discussing if girls are sexier when they are pregnant. Inquiring minds want to know, except me.

I dropped them off at their destination and they continued the discussion as they got out of the truck, neither of them thanked me but that's ok. The insight into the mind of the millennial drunk was thanks enough.

31

FIVE PEOPLE
AND A TRAIN

The same night I picked up William and his friends, I also picked up another group of 5 people from downtown Nashville. They had been out drinking all night as well, but they were more relaxed and tired. None of them were drunk, only a little tipsy. This would have been a completely normal ride, but we had a run-in with a train. While in route to their destination we came upon a train crossing where 5 cars were in front of us already waiting for the train to pass. The crossing rails were down and red lights were blinking everywhere.

The train was moving very slow and as we sat there it got slower and slower. Finally, it stopped, and we were stuck. This was a very long train and I was not about to sit there and wait, so I did a U-turn on a one-way street and drove slowly about 100 yards before I found a crossroad where I could turn. I was looking at the map on my app, trying every turn I could find in an effort to get around the train. I bet I made 5 U-turns as I navigated my way to their BnB where they were staying. Finally, I figured it out and we found an overpass that got us to the right side of the tracks. They were very thankful when I dropped them off.

Here is the rest of the story: the train was stopped for over an hour. It was so long that it was blocking every intersection in south Nashville that had train tracks. Traffic was a disaster as people all over the place were doing U-turns and attempting to get around the situation. I ended up taking a few people to the airport and by the time I was in the area again, 3 hours later, the train had disappeared. What a mess!

32

GRAYSON AND HIS DRUNK WIFE

Grayson and his wife were going to the airport, so they called a rideshare. Unfortunately, I got the request. First thing I noticed when I pulled up was the wife stumbling toward my truck. She was bombed. Grayson, on the other hand, was sober and beyond obnoxious. As we started toward the airport, Grayson asked me to stop at a gas station. He said that they were flying to Virginia and due to the high price of cigarettes in northern Virginia, he needed to stock up for his trip. I pulled into the gas station where Grayson bought two packs of cigarettes. Note to self, stocking up equals two packs.

When Grayson got back into the truck, he told me that his wife hated to fly and so her strategy was to get as drunk as possible so the flight wouldn't bother her. I don't think that is a good strategy since TSA probably stopped her from getting through security, but who knows. Honestly, that ride to the airport was one of the longest rides even though it only took about 12 minutes. The drunk wife was yammering in the back seat, slurring her words to the point that I couldn't understand anything she was saying. Grayson was telling me about his exploits as an UBER driver. *Shoot me now* I thought to myself as I watched the miles clicking down on my app. I admit I dropped them off at the very first door at the terminal. Hopefully, the wifey sobered up before TSA got a whiff of her.

33

THE DRUNK WIFE

Speaking of drunks, let me tell you about the wife of a football coach that I picked up and drove to the airport. I won't say her name or give any information about her husband because he wouldn't be happy with her if he knew about that morning. I picked her up from her secret girlfriend's house and drove her 30 miles back to her place. She too was bombed from too much alcohol. I still don't know the story about her and the girlfriend because she was Skyping with another friend for the entire duration of the ride back to her place.

Drunk people are annoying. This woman kept putting the phone in front of me and wanted me to talk to her friend on Skype. Keep in mind I am driving 70 miles an hour down the highway at 3 am. Talking on Skype was not a viable or safe option at the time. The friend on the phone was very nice and I must say, their conversation was interesting. The drunk wife kept trying to "hook me up" with the friend on the phone which was a waste of time. The friend on the phone lived on the other side of the United States and was rather annoyed that she was called so early in the morning.

When the ride was over, the drunk wife told me that I wasn't supposed to repeat anything she and I talked about with the friend on the phone. I told her that she had nothing to worry about because I don't know the friend on the phone and she and I didn't discuss anything.

I did look her up when I got home. Sure enough, she is who she said she was, and her husband is famous to some extent. Lives of the rich and famous are never a dull moment and I will say, rich people…… never tip.

34
KATY, JR, AND NANCY

You would think that when I pick up people early morning from a bar, I would be picking up drunk people who have been out all night, binging away their problems. However, sometimes the drunk person I pick up is the bartender. I picked up Katy from a bar and drove her 20 miles north to her house. Along the way she told me all about her deadbeat mother who calls the cops on her when she is out late, even though the mother lives at Katy's house. Then she told me about her sister who has been living in her garage for 2 years; no job. The life of a bartender is evidently underappreciated since Katy is supporting the whole family.

When we arrived at her home, Katy's mom was outside smoking a cigarette. It was 4 am. Katy joined her when she got out of the truck. Ah, family!

I wasn't out of Katy's driveway before I got a request to pick up JR. It took me 5 minutes to get to his house. JR got in, smelling of weed so bad that it made my eyes water. He was on his way to work where he is a glassmaker. If memory serves, making glass requires a great deal of heat. I don't think that being around heat while stoned out of your mind is a good combination.

Before I dropped off JR, Nancy was put into the queue. So, as soon as I dropped off JR at his glass company, I was already on my way to pick up Nancy. I was 5 minutes away from arriving at Nancy's house when she called me. "Good morning, I'm here in the driveway with the other rideshare driver. I will see you when you get here" she said before she up and hung up on me. That phone call seemed odd at the time, but it was just the beginning.

When I pulled into Nancy's driveway, I saw a car with its hood up and many parts laying on the driveway. Nancy was standing there with her suitcase, so I parked the truck and got out to load her bag into the back. Nancy says, "Jim meet Bob, Bob meet Jim". (Curious because I didn't know Nancy, yet she was introducing me like we were old friends) Bob was working diligently on his car which I surmised had broken down in Nancy's driveway. Bob nodded and then went back to work. Nancy got into the truck. She proceeded to tell me that Bob pulled into the driveway, loaded her luggage, and then began to pull down the driveway. The car filled with smoke, chugged a few times, and then gave up the ghost. Bob was determined to fix his own car; Nancy was determined to get to the airport.

We left Bob and 12 minutes later I was dropping Nancy off at the Southwest gate at BNA, which is short for Barry Field in Nashville, otherwise known as Nashville International Airport. I am sure Nancy had a good trip and I would bet that Bob is considering a membership with AAA. I went about my morning with 3 more rides under my belt and $55 in my pocket.

35

AMBER AND A FOGGY SITUATION

Have you ever known a person who had a fear of driving? How about the fear of thunderstorms or tornadoes? I think these are rational fears that some people have and rightly so. However, when I picked up Amber, she was afraid of fog. Let me set up the scene for you, it was foggy, and we were 3 miles away from Amber's house. For the next few minutes, Amber gripped the dashboard, leaving fingernail indentations as she told me about her history with fog. "You can't see through it and you never know what's out there. People will stop their car and you will run right into it. No one should drive in the fog" she said as she looked at me with fright. I guess I should mention, Amber was very drunk which explains much of this story. The question I asked her, "if you are scared of fog, why are you driving in the fog with a complete stranger?" "I'm tired and hungry" she admitted. Note to self: food and a pillow are always more powerful than the fear of fog.

36

FIRST RIDE "SHARE"

While people use a "rideshare" app such as UBER or LYFT, most rides are not actually "shared". Passengers request a ride but rarely share the ride with someone they don't know. LYFT has a feature that you can request a ride on your own, or for a lower fee, you can request a ride "share" which can lead the driver to pick up other passengers along the route to your destination. On the driver app, the ride will say LYFT if the ride is a passenger who wants the ride all to themselves or SHARED if the passenger is too cheap to pay for their own ride and is ok with strangers tagging along. I had completed over 500 rides before I got my first shared ride.

I was dispatched first to pick up Laquesha who was on her way to a hotel downtown. I think she worked in housekeeping. As Laquesha and I started on the journey downtown, I then got another call to pick up Rose who was only 8 blocks away. Rose got into the truck and talked to me as we drove 6 miles to the hotel. Laquesha never said a word. She sat in the backseat, focused on the phone as if it was going to spit out tonight's winning lottery numbers. Rose was very chit chatty. I dropped Laquesha off at the hotel and then proceeded to the location Rose had requested. Ultimately, I dropped her off at a customer service office in Nashville.

This was the first and only time I have ever driven two passengers at the same time who didn't know each other. I must admit, it was beyond odd. I didn't know which one I should try to talk too but I soon realized Rose is a people person, so I spent my time chatting with her. Laquesha is a laundry person. I am sure the sheets and pillowcases don't have much to say.

37

THE STUDENT-
ATHLETE

Driving kids in my truck is nothing short of annoying. I will be honest; I don't enjoy driving high school kids around town. Most of the time they are going to school but on this occasion, the kid was going someplace different. I was driving on a Wednesday morning. I started around 3 am and by 9 am I was tired of sitting in my truck. I decided I would do one more ride and then I would head home to get some breakfast, play with my dogs, and take a short nap before returning to my daily job-hunting tasks on the internet. I got a call from a rider named Tony. When I arrived, I found a high school kid walking thru his parking lot.

When he got into the truck, I asked him if he was going to School? He told me he was going to his coach's house, in Gallatin, Tennessee. I was ready to scream when I looked at the app which showed the ride would take 45 minutes to get to Gallatin, which is the opposite direction of my house. Tony never said a word during the 45-minute ride north. I ended up dropping him off at a condo which seemed suspicious to me, but it was none of my business. The part of the story that really aggravated me was that I was now over 50 miles from home and there wasn't anyone up in Gallatin who wanted to go to Nashville. So, I drove 50 miles on my own dime.

People who take rideshare should be aware of where they are going and take into consideration where the driver might live. A good financial tip for the driver at the end of a ride will go a long way with a driver who is a long way from home.

38

GUS – THE "OUT THERE" BARTENDER

Every drive is unique in its' own way, and that is about all I can say for Gus. I have picked him up two times from the same location. I remember him, but he didn't remember me on the second trip. Gus is a bartender who seems like he is perpetually stoned. He doesn't smell like pot and I don't think he ever uses pot at work, but he has this way about him that makes you wonder if he is "tripping" on something. What a nut ball.

Gus has a very good command of the English language and when you talk to him it's as if someone shoved a Thesaurus down his throat. He's an odd little bird who loves big words but never actually makes any sense. You have to love a happy person who can ramble on like a dictionary but never really get to the point. He reminded me of the two drunk guys discussing whether or not pregnant women are hot or not. Gus would ramble about why he finds it to be so fascinating to work all night and then enjoy breakfast at the 6-story diner on the corner of 2nd Ave and Demonbreun in downtown Nashville. He would ramble and ramble and ramble. Waxing poetic about breakfast is always an enjoyable conversation, if your name is Gus. If you're Gus' driver, it's really off and you can't help to keep looking at your watch to wonder how soon the ride will be over.

39

MR. BOWTIE

One thing I wish all readers would consider before making a rideshare request on their phone; take a bath and back off on the cologne or perfume. A little goes a long way.

Not to change the subject, but if you ever see a LYFT driver with the glowing emblem on their dashboard, that emblem is called the LYFT amp. The AMP allows passengers to see a LYFT driver approach and the amp will send messages during the ride such as "let's roll" and "halfway there". LYFT drivers are sent a free amp when they reach 250 rides. I was very excited when I was on my way to get passenger 250 but when I picked up the man in the bowtie, my eyes began to water. I know the astute reader might be thinking that I was crying happy tears because I would finally get my amp, but those tears were far from happy.

Mr. Bowtie got into my car and as I looked at the location, I realized I would be spending some time with him because his destination was 35 minutes away. 35 minutes is not long, in fact, most sit-coms are only 30 minutes. 35 minutes is nothing unless your eyes are BURNING because my passenger had bathed himself in so much cologne that I was reminded of going thru the gas chamber in basic training. Where was my gas mask when I needed it the most? I don't know what brand he was bathing in, but the fumes were making me dizzy.

Turns out, Mr. Bowtie is a counselor for young people. I surmised that when counseling young people, the counselor always needs to be on their guard. Don't trust anyone. I think the cloud of smell hanging around Mr. Bowtie was his primary defense to ensure no one got too close. I can't think of any other reason why a person should boil themselves in the foul stench of cheap cologne before heading into work. I will give him credit; he was extremely nice.

40
SCHOOL KIDS AND FAST FOOD

There is nothing I dislike about rideshare more than taking high school kids to school and the next few stories revolve around high school kids. When I was young I either rode the bus or caught a ride with a friend. I never in a million years would have ever dreamed about taking a cab to school, but alas this is a world where kids are entitled and operate on their time. I got a call to pick up a girl and when I arrived, two young girls came out and hopped into the truck. One was in 10th grade, the other was in 12th grade. The 12th grader immediately told me she scheduled a "STOP" along the route and then I looked to verify and sure enough, we were on our way to get the kiddies some breakfast before heading to high school. The 10th grader immediately began changing her outfit in the backseat. She didn't get undressed and I didn't pay any attention, but I know that when we arrived at their favorite fast food restaurant, she got out of the truck in a different outfit than that which she got into the truck.

We arrived at 8:26 am to the famous chicken establishment. I asked the girls as they were getting out of the truck, "What time does school start?" "8:30" they replied, "but our teachers don't mind if we are late". As they walked casually into the restaurant, I thought to myself, "YES, they really do mind if you are late!" Snot.

You must admit; kids can be snotty these days. They seem to think the world revolves around them and this is what is wrong with the younger generation. They want to show up late as if there is no problem. These are usually the kids who land a job and they are looking for a new job several months later when their employer terminates them for never showing up on time.

Anyway, the girls came back to the truck and I got them to school a few minutes later. Off they went, armed with chicken sandwiches to homeroom. Granted, they were 10 minutes late, but who's counting?

41

THE KID WHO STOLE MY GUM

Let me repeat, I do not like taking kids to high school. Most of the time they get into the truck, shove their little headphones down their ear canals as far as humanly possible, and stare at their phone because they cannot live without their phone. Occasionally, one of them speaks and I am dumbfounded for a moment. On this occasion, I picked up a brother and sister who were headed to school. The ride was about 20 minutes due to traffic. The younger sister sat in the front seat next to me while her older brother sat in the backseat behind his sister.

I should mention that the center consul of the truck has two cupholders. At all times, I have containers of gum that are made just for those cupholders. I am sure you have seen all the different brands and choices in your local grocery store checkout lane. I usually have peppermint and Bubblemint which is what I had on that day. The sister asked me if she could have a piece of gum? "Of course you may," I replied, "help yourself." She politely took a piece of peppermint and all was fine with the world. Her brother then inquired if he could have a piece of gum and I gave him the same response. I didn't pay much attention to him at the time because I was in traffic attempting to turn. When we got to the school, both of them thanked me for the ride and went off to class. I have no idea if they were on time or late, but at least I didn't have to wait at Chick-Fil-A before we got to their school.

Several rides later I reached for the peppermint gum, opened the container, and instantly remembered why I dislike high school kids. Yes, you guessed it, the container which was full at the beginning of the trip with the two kids now had 3 pieces left. That little thug in the backseat must have emptied the container quietly while I was focusing on traffic. Those containers cost about $4.99 and mine was now empty. I prayed for the rest of the day that he choked on every piece. Thief!

42

SMELLY GUY

Aside from taking many passengers to the airport each morning when I am out driving rideshare, I also take many people to work, to conventions, and to visit friends. It's not at all uncommon for people who work in the city to use rideshare because ultimately, it's cheaper than the cost of the car, gas, insurance, a car payment, and monthly parking fees. Granted there is no equity being earned in a vehicle, but the overall cost is a wash and there is far less stress when someone in the city doesn't need to worry about a car.

One morning I was dispatched to pick up a passenger whose name escapes me. He was standing outside at the pick-up point when I arrived. He got into the truck and we started making the trek from his apartment to the Gaylord convention center. The Gaylord is an extremely large convention center. The size of the hotel rivals any Las Vegas hotel although the Gaylord is not connected to a casino.

Within a minute or two, the smell from his side of the truck smacked me in the head like the crack of a whip. The body odor of this guy was worse than any NHL locker room. I could barely stand it. I turned the air on, but I couldn't decide if I should blow it on myself so I could get some fresh air, or should I blow the air on him. I panicked. I thought to myself if I blow the air on him, the smell would circulate throughout my truck and I would never get it out. It was horrible, it was blinding. I turned the air off. I held my breath while I was driving. My eyes were watering. Therefore, just for the fun of it, I asked him what he did for a living? He responded, "I'm a cook!" I cringed and thought to myself, *Gak!*

I dropped him off and immediately turned the heater on high, rolled down all the windows, and sprayed the whole truck down with my emergency can of Febreze. I drove down the highway with air blowing thru my car even though it was only 25 degrees outside. By the time I picked up my next passenger, the truck smell was back to normal and my eyes had stopped watering.

43

THE INTERVIEW WITH SARAH

If you GOOGLE colleges within the Nashville area, you will find that there are more than 20 four-year colleges in this city. This means there is an overabundance of college kids, some with participation trophies and some without. Some students find jobs in the area and some do not. Many of the students fall in love with Nashville and when it is time to graduate, they begin looking within the Nashville area for a permanent job. Some of them intern at a company and then move to a full-time position after graduation.

On a Wednesday afternoon, I was dispatched to pick up Sarah in downtown Nashville. Sarah was a very pretty girl who was dressed up as if she was ready for Church or a respectable date. When she got into the back of the truck, I said, "Hello, where are you off to today?" Sarah told me she was on her way to an interview. She seemed nervous and so I asked her if she had done many interviews in the past. She then informed me that she had never worked. Her parents provided everything for her, and she had never had a real job, but she was about to graduate with her master's degree in communications so she was doing some interviews so she could work after graduation. You have to admire the kids who have everything handed to them on a silver platter and applaud them when they attempt to enter life without the parent's credit card to support them.

I asked her if she would like me to ask her some questions to get her in the right frame of mind for the interview? Sarah agreed. For the next 15 minutes, I asked her some standard applicant questions that I always use when I am doing an interview. Sarah stumbled thru some answers that honestly made no sense. I wasn't surprised as she is young and has had everything handed to her on a silver platter in the past. She was very well spoken although, given 500 words in her retort, the question was never truly answered. I have seen this in the past where a question is asked and while the candidate rambles for 5 minutes, they never answer the question.

I hope Sarah did well in the interview. She told me the interview on this day was not a job that she really wanted, nor did she want to work in the area of Nashville where this business was located. She indicated that this area wasn't a very nice part of town and she wouldn't be happy working there. She had her heart set on a job for which she interviewed in the upscale part of town. She felt that she would be better suited in a more high-class part of Nashville. You have to admire that level of honesty in a self-absorbent graduate.

44

VANITY GIRL GOES TO THE STORE

There are some rides that will always make me laugh and the vanity girl was no exception. I received a dispatch from Kim during my first week of driving rideshare. I was still new to the whole rideshare world and I am sure I made many mistakes along the way. After accepting the ride, I headed toward the destination which was an apartment complex with a security gate. The great thing about rideshare is that after a ride is accepted, the passenger can text or call the driver to give them any instructions such as the gate code for a security gate or to ask, "Where are you, I'm running late." I received a text from Kim who stated she would meet me out front of the main building. When I arrived at the complex, I found a small parking area outside the security gate. I parked and waited for Kim to arrive.

A few minutes later a young, very attractive girl got into my truck. She was wearing a purple velour track outfit. After saying, "good morning," I headed out of the complex and toward the destination. I had to point out that she was attractive because, during the ride to the department store (her destination), Kim didn't speak two words to me. She did, however, spend the entire ride looking at herself on her phone. Sometimes women will use the rear-facing camera on their phone as a mirror to check themselves out to ensure everything is looking as it should. Kim looked and looked and looked. She took a few selfies and the looked some more. After a few minutes, I was having a hard time keeping a straight face. I have never seen someone so in love with themselves. She fixed her hair many times. She turned her head to the right, then the left, always ensuring she could see herself on the phone. She took some more pictures using a filter program of some sort. I could see, out of the corner of my eye, some pictures she took where she put little bunny ears on her head or a mouse nose on her face. Kim was fascinated with herself.

We arrived at the department store and Kim got out of the truck. She said a quick "Thank You" and went through the double doors. I am assuming she headed directly to the "mirror" department where she would see much more of her most favorite person in the whole wide world. Here's looking at you Kim!

45

WAFFLE HOUSE

This situation I will admit made me angry. It wasn't the passengers' fault; it was just circumstance that didn't go my way. I was out driving one afternoon which I don't normally do. Most of the time I drive in the morning, beginning at 3 am and ending sometime between 8 am and 10 am. However, on this day I decided to go driving in the afternoon to get a few more rides for the week. It happened that I was doing a "ride challenge" where if I did 106 rides by the end of the week, I would receive a $113 bonus. I didn't need the money but the challenge of getting 106 rides in 7 days was something I knew I could do.

I was finishing a ride with a very obnoxious woman and her two kids who were scared to death of her when I got another call added to my queue. After dropping off the obnoxious woman and then spraying my truck with a blast of Febreze, I went to pick up Cade. Again, I will mention that a driver cannot see the destination of a passenger until they arrive. When I arrived to pick up Cade, the destination said Waffle House and had a street address. I didn't think anything of this when Eric got into the vehicle with his rather large backpack. Turns out Cade was a construction worker who was staying at a friend's house during the week and was now heading home. This should have been my first clue that something was amuck.

We started toward the destination and I completely didn't pay any attention when we got on the highway heading North, keeping in mind I live 20 miles south of the location where Cade got into the truck. After a few minutes, I looked down and noticed we had 35 minutes to go until we got to the destination. I asked Cade, "which Waffle House are we going to if you don't mind me asking?" "The Waffle House in Clarksville," Cade said as I began to quietly fume inside my head.

Every minute of that trip I was getting further and further away from home. When I finally dropped off Cade at his mom's car at the Waffle House in Clarksville, Tennessee, I was 62.5 miles from home. Rideshare only pays when you have a rider in your vehicle and on a Friday evening, there was no one going from the Waffle House in Clarksville, Tennessee back to Nashville. It took me 90 minutes to get home and ultimately, I didn't make as much as you might think on the ride because I had nothing but dead time going home. I will say that when I arrived home, I had a buffalo chicken bacon sandwich waiting for me from *Jersey Mikes*. This made my day.

46
THE SECURITY GUY

You would think that in a city the size of Nashville and given a large number of rideshare drivers at all hours of the day who are out looking for their next ride, it would be uncommon to get the same rider twice. I have picked up Frank and taken him to work 5 times already.

I usually leave the house around 3 am and head for the gas station if I forgot to fill up the day before. Frank usually requests a ride to work around 3:10 am, the same time I am done at the gas station. So, it stands to reason that Frank's request would be out there the same time I am logging in for the day. Given that Frank and I are both rather regimented individuals, I have driven him to work 6 times already. In fact, I drove him to work the morning I wrote this story.

A few weeks ago, I took Frank to work in the morning and when we arrived, something happened that made both of us laugh. Frank works at a local department store and has worked there for a few years. He enjoys his job although he has mentioned that when the store is understaffed, he enjoys his job less. On this morning, we drove into the parking lot and were immediately flagged down by the new security guy who spends his time guarding the empty parking lot at night.

This guy drove up to the truck, rolled down his window, and proceeded to go into this random missive about how the store is closed and if I needed anything I would have to come back at another time. I looked at Frank, and then looked back at the security guy and said, "I'm just dropping him off to work". The security guy looked at me befuddled and drove away slowly. I then looked at Frank and said, "what's up with your boy Captain America over here, guarding the parking lot as if we just drove thru the DMZ?"

Frank laughed as he got out of the truck. He said "have a good day" as he always does and walked into the building. I drove away slowly as to not bring attention to Captain America who was back to keeping watch for unruly drivers who might think they could go shopping at a store that is usually open 24-hours. Who could dream of such a thing?

47

THE PANCAKE
COOK

I remember when I picked up Ken at his apartment complex at 4:15 am, he walked out very urgently as if he was a man on a mission. Ken was about 6'2", slim, bald, and walking with his chest puffed out as if he just went 20 rounds with a bench press. Ken was a tough guy who was either really motivated or just late to work. I think it was the latter. He jumped into the truck and blurted, "GOOD MORNING". "Ok, that was loud," I thought to myself. "Good Morning" I replied and then asked him where we were heading? Ken told me he was heading to work, so I put the truck in drive and off we went. Ken sat in the back seat on the passenger side. I asked him where he worked, and he told me for the past several years he was a "chef" at a local breakfast establishment. I don't want to say the name of the restaurant, but it turned out to be a popular pancake restaurant.

For the next 15 minutes, the truck was quiet with regard to the conversation, but Ken was breathing so heavy in the back seat that I would have sworn he was doing his best Darth Vader imitation. He was looking at his phone but breathing so loud that I began to think there may have been something wrong with him. After a few minutes of listening to him gargle, pant and make heavy breathing sounds, I asked him how he was doing? "I'M GOOD" he blurted again. He was a very motivated man.

When we arrived at the restaurant, Ken thanked me and hopped out of the truck. With chest puffed out and his arms propped up by some imaginary struts, he walked with vigor into the pancake place. I am sure he was breathing heavy as I turned to see if I needed to wipe down the seats, the window, the door, or the center consul in the truck. I sprayed Febreze in the back and headed to my next call. Hopefully, Ken didn't pass out in the pancake batter.

Have you noticed that I seem to use a ton of air freshener? I am seeing a reoccurring theme.

48

BOOTY CALL

Although there are many reasons to call a rideshare, sometimes the original reason a passenger destination can change mid-ride. For example, a passenger may want to go to a friend's house, but during the ride, they decide they are hungry and thus they change the destination from the friend's house to McDonald's or the local "stop-and-rob," otherwise known as the minimart. When I picked up Greg from downtown Nashville, this is what happened, so to speak.

Greg requested a ride around 4 am. He had been out drinking all night and decided that after an 8-hour binge it was time to head home. Unfortunately, I got the ride request. I was only a few minutes away from having just dropped off another passenger in the downtown area. I pulled up to a bar on Broadway and Greg got in. The first thing I asked him was why he was wearing his arm in a sling? He told me that he had been doing bench press and although he hadn't done any "MAX" bench in a while, he thought it was time. He said he "easily beat his old record" but after 2 reps, he heard something pop in his chest. The doctor said he heard his pectoralis tendon rip. Fun times Greg. Then he told me that he was at a Diner of some sort before I arrived, though I didn't see any food establishments in the immediate vicinity. He told me about his night of drinking all over the downtown area as we headed North. Again, I often forget to look at how far away the passenger is heading, and in this case, Greg was traveling 20 miles North to Nashville. I really didn't want to go that far because I knew I wouldn't find a passenger up in that area who wanted to come back to Nashville at 5 am, so I will admit I was not happy at all.

However, to my fortune, Greg realized he had an "acquaintance" who didn't live far away, in fact, her home was along our route. He decided that instead of going home, he would call his friend to see if she was awake. Sure enough, she answered the phone. I had to hold back my nausea as I listened to him sweet talk her into letting him come over for some morning calisthenics of the sexual nature. When he hung up the phone he exclaimed, "I just saved your ass".

To be honest, my ass didn't feel any different, but I, in turn, exclaimed, "Cool"! Greg quickly changed the destination on the rideshare app so it would direct me to his friend's house. Greg did just that and viola, the 25-minute ride became a 6-minute ride. I was very happy now because I could stay in the Nashville area, spend less time with Greg, and possibly get another ride in the area.

When we arrived in the neighborhood where Greg's friend lived, I was astonished at the size of these houses. I don't know what this woman did for a living, but her enormous house was a pretty good indication that she did well for herself.

We pulled into the driveway and Greg proceeded to tell me that I couldn't leave until he made it through the front door. Evidently, this woman, while being rather well off, has a tendency of taking Greg's calls and then falling asleep before she unlocks her front door. I'm going out on a limb here, but I think Greg has done this before. Greg didn't realize that not only did I have no intention of waiting for him, but I also had another passenger in the queue that was waiting for me. Nonetheless, the front door was open. As I backed out of the driveway, I saw Greg disappear inside the rich woman's house. Way to go Greg.

49

SPEEDING THROUGH THE PARK

I will not sit here and tell you that I am a saint, in fact, I have too many flaws to count. Some of them that come to mind when I am driving LYFT or UBER include failing to look at the time to the location such as my ride with Greg to his booty call or Eric to the Waffle House. I have also been known to push the speed limit from time to time. One such time would be my very first week as a rideshare driver. I had just dropped off a passenger and I was heading out of his neighborhood. I zigged here and zagged there. I figured eventually I would find a main road and be on my way. I was traveling down a road near the river going a modest 35 miles an hour when I saw blue lights in my rear-view mirror. There is nothing more depressing than being pulled over by a cop on a Friday night, even though I was having a very good night financially.

The cop came up to my window and asked me if I knew how fast I was going. I replied, "35ish, was that too fast?" The answer was YEP, I was in a park and didn't know it. The posted speed limit was 20.

"Officer, I had no idea I was in a park, so I'm guilty," I confessed to the short little bald cop at my window. I never saw any speed limit sign but according to the cop, I drove past 3 of them. Ok, I'm no saint so whatever. The cop took my license and went back to his car. A few minutes later he came back and told me that he was letting me off with a warning. I asked him to show me the most convenient route out of the park. He told me to keep going straight but to take it slow. I did just that. In 5 minutes, I was out of the park and my rideshare app was flashing at me again. It was now time to get another passenger and continue with my evening. Close call!

50

HAVING A BABY, BUT TAKING A RIDESHARE

By now I am sure you have noticed that the situations a rideshare driver can run into are always strange in their own right. Very rare is the ride that is completely normal and boring. Every passenger is unique in their own way. Some head to the airport, some of them head to work. When I picked up Kyle, he was just heading to work.

I should tell you that when my app started to blink at me, asking me to accept the ride from Kyle, it directed me to a satellite office of a local medical center. I didn't think twice about this because I take people to that place every other day. Most of the time I am either dropping someone off at work or picking someone up who just got off work.

When Kyle got in, he told me he was heading home and then he had to go to work. Did I mention he was heading to work? I may have forgotten to mention his wife was having a baby. She was admitted to the medical center and was in the early stages of labor. Kyle stayed with her for a while but then he had to go to work. So, he called a rideshare, went home to shower and change, and then he was heading to work. Unfortunately, I don't know how the story ended but I hope his wife gave birth after Kyle's shift was over. That is the least she could have done for him.

51

THE CHAPERONE

It was a Saturday morning and I was leaving my house. I turned on the rideshare app as I pulled out of the driveway and immediately, I received a request which I happily accepted. The request was for Shondra who was located less than 2 miles from my house. It was around 3 am when I pulled into the driveway. Shondra came out to the truck along with 3 other individuals. A very large guy sat in the front seat while Shondra and the other two individuals sat in the back. When we were on our way, I realized the ride would take over 30 minutes as we were headed north of Nashville.

Shondra was definitely in charge of the group. I don't know what her role was with the other three, but it seemed as if she was their chaperone and was going along with them to ensure all three of them got back to Tennessee State University without incident. I could be wrong, but she seemed as if she was responsible to get them home safely. The ride was quiet as I entered the highway but the quiet didn't last long. The very large guy sitting next to me decided to fall asleep, rock his head back, and snore. This kid could have been an alternate on the Olympic snoring team. I thought he was going to inhale the vinyl off the dashboard. There is nothing worse than being in a car with 4 sleeping people, one of which smells bad and snores so loud you can't hear yourself think. He was epic in size and volume. 20 miles I had to listen to him, wanting to open the door and push him out as soon as possible.

Share My Ride

When we arrived at Tennessee State University, I heard "uh oh" from the backseat. This is never a good thing to hear. It turns out Shondra left her ID back at the house where she first got into my truck. The ride cost her $30 to which I kept $18. It would have cost her another $60 if I had taken her all the way back to get her ID and then returned her to the exact location we were at when she realized her mistake. She didn't have that kind of money, so she got out with the two people in the backseat and the snoring creature sitting beside me. It was not a good way to start her day, but she did a good job of ensuring the three students made it back to campus. Hopefully, she got her ID returned to her without incident and I hope the large guy enrolled in a sleep study.

52

DON'T CALL 911, CALL RIDESHARE?

I was dispatched on a Saturday morning to pick up David. David lived in a small house about 10 miles south of Nashville. It took me about 4 minutes to get to his home once I received the dispatch. David got into the truck and I said, "Good Morning, where are we headed this morning?" David told me I was taking him to the emergency room. Between you and me, it seems odd to take a rideshare to the emergency room, but we all have to make choices in life.

I asked David why we were heading to the emergency room, which happened to be 12 miles away? He said he was having heart palpitation, was sweating and couldn't sleep. I told him that it may be a better idea to call an ambulance. David then told me the last time an ambulance was called it took 15 minutes to arrive and then it would take another 15 minutes to get to the hospital. He said when he looked at his rideshare app, he noticed the closest driver (me) was only 4 minutes away and since we were already driving, chances were that I could get him to the hospital faster than the ambulance.

I began to ask him about his symptoms because when you are driving on backroads in the middle of the night, there is nothing better to do than to act as a physician/investigator. David told me that he had been drinking at a local bar and he thought someone slipped something into his drink. That's a plausible excuse for heading to the emergency room, so we proceeded. However, I wasn't finished with my interrogation.

I asked David what he had been drinking. He told me he didn't drink alcohol, instead, he drank Coke. He said he was hanging out with friends and lost track of the time; the time being 8 hours at the bar. Now, common sense would say that if anyone was drinking Coke for 8 hours, they would have a very high amount of caffeine in their system which explains why David couldn't sleep. David also told me that earlier that day, his father had been placed on life support at the local hospital. I can't remember the reason his father had fallen ill, but the life support was a temporary measure as his prognosis wasn't good.

So, here was David, strung out on caffeine and the knowledge of knowing his father is dying and it's 4 am. I was thinking David was having a small panic attack and needs nothing more than some water, time, and a paper bag. This made me feel better that he didn't call the ambulance which would have cost significantly more than taking a rideshare to the hospital so he could sit there for a few hours to calm down. Hopefully, David made it through the night and the hospital bill didn't set him back too many months because I am sure he had a very large Coke tab to pay at the bar each weekend.

Let's toast to David's good health and the memory of his father.

53

THE SLEEPY GIRL

One night I was working on a Friday night. I think I have mentioned that I don't usually drive the night shift but every now and then it's good to mix things up. I had dropped off someone at their condo when a "bonus area" popped up on the app. Lucky for me I was in the bonus area, so I kept the truck in park, and I watched the bonus money start to come in.

When a rideshare driver is in a bonus area, the bonus starts small but increases every 5 seconds. It only increases a few cents, but if you wait long enough, the cents can add up. I have waited in a bonus area before where it started at $2 and by the time I got my next ride request, the bonus was over $10 which is tacked on to the fare for the next ride. The bonus is paid by the rideshare company rather than the passenger.

Anyway, the bonus had worked its way up to $4 when the next request came through on my phone and after hitting 'accept' I was on my way. I was only a few blocks away and it didn't take long to arrive at a very nice condo where 8 people were coming out of the building. Two people got into my truck, 4 people got into their own SUV, and another UBER car pulled up and two people got into that car. Sadly, everyone was going to the same destination. I don't know why it took so many vehicles, but so be it. A very drunk girl got into my passenger seat while her boyfriend got into the backseat. As we pulled away, she put her head on the center consul of my truck and went to sleep. Far be it for me to judge, but if someone is so drunk that they need a nap before they go to the bar, perhaps they shouldn't go to the bar?

The woman slept during the 2-minute ride to the bar. Personally, I would have walked but a ride is a ride. When we got to the bar, the woman stumbled out of my vehicle, tripped over the curb and was caught on the way down by her boyfriend. Kudos to him for being her knight in shining armor.

54
NOT ENOUGH SEATBELT

I know there are some very large individuals in this world, but I picked up a security guard who was so large, he ran out of seatbelt. It was an early Sunday morning and I picked up this guy who was heading downtown Nashville. I remember when he approached the truck thinking to myself, *Wow, that man is huge*. He opened the door and asked me if he could sit in the front. I reached over and slid the seat back as far as it would go. He climbed into the truck slowly, filling the entire passenger seat space. My guess is this man weighed well over 400 lbs. We couldn't get the seatbelt around him. We pulled it all the way out and it barely reached the clasp. Since we were going only a short distance, he decided to skip the seatbelt.

I drove slowly. I give him credit for going to work every day, but I also feel bad for him because his breathing was so labored, I feel he had some serious health issues. We arrived downtown and he got out of the truck. I am not kidding when I tell you the truck was leaning in his direction when he got out and I watched him walk into his place of employment. That was one, incredibly large man.

55

AN ADDICT AND HIS BEAR SUIT

Cravings are a pain in the butt sometimes, especially when you get a craving at 3 am and you don't have a car. This is when you request a rideshare and some idiot like me shows up at 3:05 am to take you to the gas station so you can take care of that craving. I got a call from Chris, and after I hit accept, I clicked on his picture because at first glance because something was odd. Chris uploaded a selfie of himself wearing a bear costume. This is how he wants the public to perceive him from what I guess. What does it say about a person who wants to show off to the world wearing a bear costume?

When I picked up Chris, we were headed to the gas station for cigarettes. He began to tell me about being at the hospital all night with his uncle who was addicted to drugs. Chris came home and found him unresponsive on the floor. 911 was called and the ambulance showed up to take his uncle to the hospital where he was in stable condition.

We arrived in 3 minutes and he disappeared inside to buy a $12 pack of cigarettes. The ride cost him $15 of which I got $9. So, in total, he spent $27 for one pack of cigarettes. I think it's ironic that he was buying cigarettes to cope with a situation with his uncle who was an addict. I didn't have the heart to explain to him that if he is spending $27 on cigarettes at 3 am, he himself is an addict; an addict who enjoys portraying himself in a bear costume. What goes around comes around.

56

THE BOTTLE
OF WINE

I was out driving early morning and got a call from a hotel near the airport. I picked up Roger who was quite a character. His arms were covered with full sleeve tattoos which were phenomenal. When he got into the truck, he told me he was heading downtown to a friend's house for a few hours before heading to the airport. Roger was in town to set up an art exhibit for his company. He comes to town, sets up the exhibit and then returns home. I am not sure how we got on the topic, but we started discussing relationships and how to make a relationship last. It happened to be my wedding anniversary which furthered the conversation. The conversation was fun and it helped pass the time it took to drive him to his destination. When we arrived, he asked me if he could give me a tip? I of course, accept all forms of cash. However, I didn't get cash. Roger handed me a brand-new bottle of wine and told me to go home and toast my marriage. He got out of the truck and disappeared, as I sat there looking at this bottle of wine. First of all, I don't drink wine. Second, where was he hiding this? He had a small backpack with him so obviously, he had this bottle stashed in his bag. However, I still thought to myself, *who carries around a bottle of wine at 4 am in their backpack?* I put the bottle in the center consul of the truck to keep it safe and I went about my day. Turns out, the bottle was worth $20. It wasn't cash, but it's the thought that counts. Thanks Roger!

57

ALEXANDER AND HIS BURGER

When driving late at night, I am bound to pick up some passengers who have had too much alcohol, too much pot, or both. When I picked up Alexander, he acted as if he was stoned out of his mind although I didn't smell any pot which I can usually pick up quite easily. When people smoke pot, they tend to get the munchies. Alexander had the "munchies" which was evident by the hamburger he was carrying with him. He spoke very highly about his hamburger, apologizing that he didn't bring one for me. I have learned to accept the notion that it's the thought that counts. 3 minutes later, I dropped off Alexander who couldn't wait to eat his burger. I hope it lived up to the hype.

I mention this story because I picked up a woman the other night from a bar who got into my car with a giant hot dog smothered in onions. The smell of onions can permeate a car and this incident made my car smell like a sub shop. She managed to drop pieces of onion on the floor, under the seat which made my car stink. Never again will I allow anyone to get into my vehicle with onions. At least Alexander kept his burger in its wrapper until we got to his house. Kudos to him, thumbs down to her.

58

DAVID THE DRUMMER

The drive of shame is what I call it when I pick up someone who is on their way home from having sex with someone. I can always tell because their clothes are a bit disheveled, they smell like sweat, and often they flat out tell me about their adventures. This was the story of David who was in town with a band. I will keep the name of the band a secret for their own privacy and to spare them the humiliation. David sent a ride request and I picked him up in front of a pizza shop.

Evidently, he picked up a girl at the bar where the band was performing, and they took a rideshare back to her place which was located on top of the pizza place. I would guess the smell of pizza wouldn't put you in the "mood," but David must enjoy the smell of cheese while the girl clearly needed some pepperoni.

I drove David back to the bar where his band performed and there was the tour bus. David was running late. For anyone who doesn't know, when a band is on tour, they keep a very rigid departure schedule late at night when traveling from city to city. I know this because I am related to a famous drummer who will remain nameless, but he knows who he is. David got on the bus, smelling like sex and pizza and away he went on to another town and another pizzeria.

59

THE LOST CAR

I left early one morning and within a few seconds after pulling out of my driveway I got a ride request from Kendra. It was 2:45 am and Kendra lived only 5 miles from me, so it didn't take me any time at all to arrive at her house. This was her first-time using rideshare. I know this because I got a message on my phone stating, "This is Kendra's first ride". When I picked her up, she told me that a friend had borrowed her car but didn't return it. She had to be at work at 9:30 am and so we were going to her friend's house to see if the car was there. This seemed a bit strange given it was 3 am, but we headed to the friend's house. When we got to her friend's house there was no sign of her car. Kendra then put in another address and we went there looking for her car, but again we did not find it. Kendra was a bit frustrated, so we headed back to her place and the ride was over.

When I pulled up to her house, Kendra asked me if she could tip me in cash. I always accept all forms of cash you know. Kendra quickly laid two bills on my center consul and then dashed out of the truck and into her house. I put the bills in my pocket and went to my next ride request. It was very dark in the truck because it was now 3:25 am and Kendra's neighborhood was not well lit.

A few rides later, I was standing outside my truck waiting for the passenger to bring me their suitcases which were sitting on the front porch when I arrived. As I stood there, I reached into my pocket and pulled out the two bills that happened to be $20's. That sweet Kendra tipped me $40 for running her around at 3 am in her effort to find her car. I will tell say this; you just never know what to expect from people. This was the largest tip I have received to date. I hope Kendra made it to work on time.

60

THE SUBSTITUTE WHO COULD'T READ CURSIVE

I want to stay away from politics and my views on the world when I am driving a passenger to their destination. However, sometimes that is a hard thing to do. I got a ride request from David and when I picked up David at his home, he informed me I was taking him to school.

David was a substitute teacher who was running late due to a problem with his pants. He told me that a button had fallen off his pants and therefore he had to borrow a pair of pants from his friend who brought him a pair of pants to his home. Personally, I think David should own more than one pair of pants, but I digress. I asked David why he didn't simply sew the button back on his pants which would have been much fast. He told me that he didn't know how to sew.

This sparked a conversation about home economics and the fact that many schools do not teach it anymore. I used to love Home Ec. because I learned to sew, and I learned to cook. I will admit that I wasn't very good back then because I replaced a tablespoon of sugar for a tablespoon of salt when making a coffee cake. It wasn't pretty. Anyway, David never took Home Economics in school.

He then told me that he also never learned to read cursive writing. They don't teach cursive in many schools and that includes the school where David went for elementary school. He told me that his grandmother sends him greetings cards every year with a message written in cursive, but he can never read it.

I don't want to get on a soapbox, but what kind of substitute teacher can't read cursive and can't sew a button on his pants? No offense to David, but those are life skills that all teachers should know and life skills that all schools should teach. We need less sensitivity training and common core math, and we need more life skills taught in school such as sewing, balancing a checkbook, and self-awareness. That's just my opinion. I feel bad for David's grandmother because her messages of love are never received.

61

ELIAS THE GREAT

I will be honest; I am not a fan of picking up kids and taking them to school. I know I have already mentioned this a time or two in this book. I would rather be picking up people who are going to the airport but that obviously can't happen on every ride. I got a call to pick up Elias. When I arrived, this short kid came out of the house. He looked like he was 12 or 14 years old. I would guess him to be no taller than 5 foot.

When he got into the truck, I confirmed the pick-up and off we went. The ride included a stop and a final destination that was over 20 miles away. I remember sighing because that is a long way to take a kid to school. I asked Elias where the first stop was because all I could see was a street address. I figured it was either a fast food restaurant or a gas station; two popular stops among the kids who take a rideshare in the morning. He told me it was a gas station. I then asked him if he was going to school and he sighed as he said, "yes!"

I then asked him what grade he was in? This question offended him because he snapped back in a rather harsh tone, "I'm in college." I was very surprised by this but then again, I did watch Doogie Howser when I was a kid.

We arrived at the gas station and little Elias went in and got himself something to drink and a bag of chips. When he returned, we headed for school. The next 20 minutes were quiet in the sense that Elias never said another word. However, I could hear the lyrics to the song he was blasting in his earphones above my radio and the road noise from being on the highway. I can't imagine how loud that music was in his ears if I could understand the lyrics over the sounds of the truck and my own radio.

Funny thing, we didn't go to school. The destination Elias put into the app was another apartment complex. Here I was, anxiously waiting to see what college we were going to as I drove 20 minutes, only to pull into an apartment complex. It was such a letdown. Elias got out of the truck and said, "Thanks" as he walked toward the building on my left.

This is what really made me laugh. I had to drive forward about 50 yards to turn the truck around. Two kids were walking down the sidewalk. I rolled down my window and asked them if they knew Elias? They did. So, I asked them what college he went too? They started laughing as they told me he was in 9th grade.

Busted! I love it when I'm right.

62

THE IMPOUND LOT

I picked up a guy who was on his way to the impound lot. He and his wife share a vehicle. She drove it to the impound lot because she works there. When he gets off work each day, he takes a rideshare to the lot to get the car and then heads home. When his wife is ready to come home, he goes back and picks her up in their car. It's a pretty good routine that works well for them.

What makes this story interesting is my own ignorance with regards to an impound lot in a city the size of Nashville. I figured there might be 20 or 30 cars in the impound lot only to find there were hundreds and hundreds of cars in the lot. This guy told me that in Nashville they impound as many as 75 cars a week for drunk driving, hit and run, and other traffic violations. He also said that for while vehicles can be towed for parking violations, those vehicles do not end up in the impound lot. The impound fee is $350 plus $40 per day that the vehicle sits in the lot. Those fines can grow to be fairly significant. If a car stays in the lot too long, it goes up for auction.

The moral of this story: **don't drink and drive**. Take a rideshare back to your home. Be safe. Paying $20 for an UBER or LYFT is much better than paying the fines involved if caught drinking and driving.

63
REDHEAD NAMED HOLLY

Drunk people are always fun as was the case with Holly. She sent a ride request and it came to my phone. Unfortunately, Holly was downtown in the busiest part of the town. Finding people on Broadway Ave downtown is never any fun. Luckily, it was 4 am and the crowds had dispersed. When I pulled up to the curb, I didn't know where exactly Holly was, but I could tell by the little icon on the phone that she was close. I thought she was across the street. I sat by the curb with my flashers on and I was sure Holly would show up soon.

As I sat there waiting patiently, a very nice-looking redhead was sucking face with a guy on the curb not far from the truck. She may as well have been licking his stomach given how far she was driving her tongue down his throat. It was quite a spectacle. When she finally came up for air, she turned and got into the truck. Sure enough, the redhead was Holly. Go figure!

I said, "Good morning. How are you this morning?"

"Tired" she replied, "ready for bed".

I then asked, "Was that your boyfriend?"
She replied, "I have no idea who he was".

While I remember blinking a few times, I didn't have any reply. Seriously, I was speechless.......

64
TWO SWEDISH GUYS

I should tell you about the two Swedish guys I picked up as I was almost finished with this book. These guys were hilarious. I picked them up at the diner on 2nd and Demonbruen where I have picked up many other riders. When I arrived, several police cars had blocked the intersection and the side street with their blue lights flashing. The two Swedes jumped into my truck. I immediately asked them, "What's going on with the police". Their response was very funny. As you read their response, I would recommend you say it out loud with your best Swedish accent.

The first Swede told me, "Two crack dealers, dancing around like chickens. You Americans be funny. They danced around, yelling at each other, and ended up knocking themselves out without ever hitting each other". The second Swedish guy jumped in, "it was like watching Dancing with Stars. We waited for them to throw a punch, but they never did. They never touched each other yet they laid each other out. Laying there like a bunch of stupids". That last comment alone made me laugh. I drove the Swedish guys to their Airbnb and that was the end of the story. The ride was normal, but the intro was memorable. They were very nice and truly made me laugh.

65

STLYLIN' AND PROFILIN'

I am not sure if profiling was a part of this story so I will let you be the judge. I got a call from Tiffany at 2 am. She was waiting outside when I pulled up to her place. I couldn't tell when she got in if she was in a bad mood, but after a few minutes of conversation, I can assure you she was not happy. I asked her where we were heading, and she replied that she "wasn't really sure" because I would be dropping her off on the side of the highway. This was perplexing until she gave me context for the rest of the story.

Her boyfriend was heading to work about 30 minutes prior to Tiffany calling me. He was an African American male who was caught speeding in his brand new, bright colored Corvette. To make matters worse, he didn't have his license with him because he walked out of his condo without his wallet. So, the police caught this guy speeding, brand new car, no license, 2 am, etc. etc. You get the picture? The police told him that if he couldn't get someone to bring his license to the scene, they would arrest him and impound his car. If memory serves, that would be a $350 impound fee plus $40 a day. I give the cops *kudos* because they ended up waiting 30 minutes at the scene for me and Tiffany to arrive. That shows a great deal of patience on their part.

Sure enough, Tiffany and I found the police with their lights on, on the side of the highway with the corvette. Tiffany's boyfriend called her and told her that I should park in front of the police, not behind them. So, I put my flashers on as I got close to the scene, pulled in front of the police, and Tiffany got out. Prior to letting her out, I asked her if she would need a ride home? She told me that from now on, the car was hers and she would drive him to work.

She didn't want him to buy the car and told him that eventually he would get pulled over for speeding. Tiffany was correct! I have a feeling that bright colored car is either going back to the dealer or will be up for sale by the end of the week. Hopefully, Tiffany's boyfriend avoided jail time although I would guess that he has a few more points on his license.

66
TWO PRIVATE PILOTS

Sometimes the people I meet doing rideshare are simply interesting. There is no odd story involved, no strange behavior, just ordinary people who need a ride. One morning I was dispatched downtown to a hotel where I picked up two individuals who were standing out front waiting for me when I arrived. I loaded their bags in the back of the truck and off we went to their destination. They were both pilots who fly a private plane for the owner of the hotel where they stayed the night before.

Their destination was a small, private airport that I didn't know existed. As a former military pilot, I asked them all kinds of questions on our ride to their aircraft. The conversation was very interesting and made me remember how much fun it is to fly above the clouds. Sometimes, the beauty of rideshare is that the conversations make you remember things from your past. Sometimes these are good memories, sometimes bad memories. But it's amazing that if you stop and listen to other people and hear their stories, you will remember things you haven't thought about in years.

I dropped them off 15 minutes after I picked them up. They got out and went on their way to their plane. There was nothing about the ride that was out of the ordinary, but I still remember the conversation.

67

THE MISSING
FRIEND

Not every story is a happy story. When I picked up Maddie on Broadway (unofficially called honkytonk row) she was distressed. She got in and I asked her how her night was going but I was not ready for the reply. Maddie was here visiting Nashville with some friends. One of her friends went missing and Maddie couldn't find her. She wasn't answering her phone. Then Maddie tells me a guy was following them around that night and she was worried that the last time she saw her friend, she was talking to this guy who was, more or less, stalking them. Maddie went back to their Airbnb to look for her, but the friend never showed up. Maddie was panicked because her friend has a habit of turning off her cell phone.

When I dropped off Maddie at her Airbnb, 3 police cars were waiting for her. Maddie had called them prior to calling me with the intent of filing a missing person's report. I told her to have the police attempt to ping her phone. Perhaps they could locate her.

For all the readers of this book, the moral of this story is to keep your phone on when you travel. Be careful if you decide to go off with a stranger. Make sure your friends know where you are and what your game plan is before you disappear in a strange city. The world is not safe and it's better to be safe than sorry. Unfortunately, I don't know how the story ends. I did watch the news and read the police blotter report for several days after this all happened, but I never saw anything about the friend. I would guess and I hope that the friend was passed out somewhere and when she woke up, the first thing she did was call Maddie.

68
JESSIE

The same morning I picked up Maddie, I picked up another rather depressed passenger. I got a call to pick up George, however, when I arrived, Jessie got into the truck. I really wish that when people requested rides for someone else, they would text the driver to give them a heads up. Anyway, Jessie was on her way to the airport to fly to Belize. I am thinking that it would be a really fun trip to go to Belize. Jessie told me she was there 4 weeks prior for vacation, but she was returning due to family reasons. It turns out her brother found out he was terminal with cancer and only had a few weeks to live. Jessie was going back to say goodbye. I am sure by the time I write this he will have passed on and hopefully is finding peace in a better world. I will keep Jessie in my prayers for the weeks and months ahead.

69

A.J. THE CONSTRUCTION GUY

Let me tell you this, there is nothing better than starting your day by meeting a construction worker who stinks to high heaven but has great prospects. I got a call to pick up AJ and when I arrived, AJ was standing in the street waiting for me. He got into the front seat and the stench of 100 zombies quickly penetrated my F-150. There were not enough air fresheners in the world the overtake the stench that was now permeating my poor truck. I was going to have to wash my seat covers when I got home. AJ was putrid in every sense of the word. He was rather large, grimy, smelly, and loud.

I said, "Good Morning" and he replied, "GOOD MORNING!!!" I was not ready for such a rambunctious response. Then I asked him, "where are we going?" He responded in a very loud, emphatic tone, "TROJAN". No, it's not what you may be thinking. Trojan is a temp agency in Nashville. AJ works for them from time to time, cleaning up after construction crews have finished building whatever project they are building at the time. Construction crews are all over

Nashville, so this job is important. To put it simply, AJ is a glorified janitor and he seemed to enjoy his work and I give him props for that. However, this story gets better.

AJ continued stridently telling me about his job and the importance of his job. He then told me while he enjoyed the temp work, his goal was to open up his own business. Keep in mind, the guy is basically yelling at me. Perhaps he had a hearing problem. I asked him what kind of business would he aspire to open? You could have given me a million guesses and I would still have never got this one right.

"Yard figurines" he thundered. "I think that business is taking off and I think I would be good at selling cement statues for people's yards," he said as I was trying to keep from looking confused. I asked him, "Would you carry gazing balls?" He then says, "What's a gazing ball?" AJ, I think you have some research to do before you spend your life fortune on the yard figurine business.

When I dropped off AJ, I sprayed my vehicle down with two different types of air freshener and then drove to my next stop with all the windows down. The heater was cranking, and my eyes were no longer watering. All is good with the world. I am sure I will think about AJ every time I look at my purple gazing ball which has been in my yard for over a decade.

70

FIVE BRIDESMAIDS IN A TRUCK

Anyone who lives in Nashville, Tennessee knows that this town is the bachelorette capital of the US. I actually "Googled" this topic and found it hard to believe that Nantucket ranked higher than Nashville on someone's list of favorite bachelorette party places. No one on this earth would ever believe that, but research is a cruel mistress at times. Let me walk you through a typical bachelorette party in Nashville. They all start out wild and crazy. However, by the end of the night, the person who planned the whole thing is pissed off that the whole night didn't go exactly to plan. Most of the group is angry at the one girl who met a guy and left with him to go have sex. The rest of the group will never let her live it down. And finally, you have the bride to be who is ultimately bored and wanting to go home to her fiancé. Anyway, I got a ride request from Nancy. It took me about 5 minutes to pull into the cul-de-sac where I picked up Nancy and her party.

Nancy was a rather large woman who sat in the front seat and her 5 bridesmaids climbed into the backseat of the truck. Luckily, the bridesmaids were all the size of your average Twizzle stick. Who knew you could get 7 people into an F-150? The ride was only 8 minutes from their home to the downtown area where the partying was expected to last all night. This group was certainly loud and boisterous. I didn't have any beverages or anything else festive in the truck at the time other than Bubblemint gum. Nancy was large and in charge and I will admit, she was extremely nice. This group made me laugh for an entire 8 minutes until I dropped them off at their downtown at honkytonk row. Their goal was to get hammered and not pay for any drinks; typical bachelorette playbook in Nashville.

I am still to this day surprised that 5 people can fit in the backseat of my truck. I have two dogs who weigh 33 pounds combined, and they do a pretty good job of taking up the whole backseat on long car trips. But anyway, I hope Nancy got married and is enjoying her life as a newlywed. Hopefully, her husband is a very patient man because I got a distinct feeling that Nancy is going to be a handful.

71

THE LIGHT-UP LYFT PLACARD

Time out. Can anyone explain to me why I have seen two LYFT light up placards in the front window of 2 different 18-wheelers heading down the highway? I am not talking about the LYFT AMP that drivers get when they complete 250 rides. I am talking about the generic LYFT light-up placard that can be purchased on Amazon for about $10. Rookies use these before they have enough rides to get their AMP. Yes, I have the placard and yes, I purchased it from Amazon for about $10. Now explain to me why a tractor-trailer would need one?

I would always recommend to any passenger that they confirm the driver's name before getting into their vehicle. The passenger's safety should always be paramount to the passenger and the driver.

72

THE 3 AM
BOOTY CALL

After you have been driving rideshare for a few days, you can quickly tell what is going on when a passenger gets into your vehicle. For example, when I pick up two people with suitcases, there is a good probability they are heading to the airport. When I pick up someone with an orange vest, yellow hard hat and a lunch box, chances are they are going to a construction site. Some of them may even dream of little cement gnomes in their yard. Keeping these conclusions in mind, when a girl gets into the backseat and says she is going to "visit a friend" at 3 am and she sneaks out of her house so she won't wake up her parents, this is code for a booty call.

Now, that being said, when I picked up Amber at 3 am I got a sorted story about going to see the best friend of her boyfriend who was being a jerk. She was taking a rideshare so if her boyfriend drove by the house, he would see her car in the driveway. She also told me that by taking a rideshare, her boyfriend would never find out that she was going to see his best friend to "talk" at 3 am in the morning. I wasn't buying her story. However, the ride was 17 minutes and she never stopped talking the entire ride. I listened, but never had a chance to get a word in or ask a question (not that I wanted to know any more than I already knew.)

The "friend" was waiting for her when we arrived. He was in a bathrobe, smoking a cigarette on the driveway. What a fine male specimen. I am sure they had an in-depth discussion about the boyfriend. Don't you?

73

MICAH AND HIS OUTFIT

This is another of my favorite stories. Using my best imagination, I couldn't have come up with this story from scratch. In fact, this story still makes me scratch my head. I got a call to pick up Micah. When I was driving down Micah's street looking at the numbers on the mailbox, I noticed Micah from about 100 yards away. He was standing in the road and his shorts lit up like a Christmas tree as they reflected the headlights on my truck. I am thinking to myself, "what on earth is this kid wearing?"

Micah got into the front seat. He looked like he hadn't combed his hair in a month and his sideburns were these gross patches of hair on his face. He looked like he had mange and was in need of a bath. However, those pants were truly scary. Fact is, they weren't pants, they were shorts. And to make matters worse, they were swim trunks. If you're wondering why they caught the light, that's because they were patterned with giant hot dogs and hamburgers. The hotdogs printed on these shorts were about 6 inches long. The hamburgers were about 4 inches by 5 inches. These were the ugliest swim trunks I have ever seen. I still have nightmares about those shorts when I think about it.

Then I asked Micah where we were going as I always ask every rider who gets into my vehicle. "I'm going to work" he replies. I then asked him, "what kind of work do you do?"

"I work in customer service," he says as I am trying to keep a straight face. Fortunately for the general public, those shorts are never seen because Micah sits in a cube at work and answers the phone at a call center. To this day, those are the ugliest shorts I have ever seen.

74
TRUE TALENT

One thing you will never hear me say, "I've seen it all". I will never see it all. Every day I see things that make me stop in my tracks. Some people are funny, some are normal, some are smelly, but some have true talent. I tell you I am not making this up, I really saw this happen.

I was sitting in bumper to bumper traffic on I24. The traffic on that highway in the morning can rival the traffic in any major city. As I slowly inched forward, I was noticing people slowly creeping by at their own pace. Some of them were texting, others were eating. Many were talking on the phone, but the lady in front of me was possibly the most talented and yet scariest people I have ever seen. I don't know her name, but I know talent when I see it. Anyway, I was sitting there watching the vehicle ahead of me and I saw this foot come up on the left side of her steering wheel. I thought she was putting on a sock. A minute later, I saw a foot come up on the right side of the steering wheel with the same action as that of the left foot. Her body then starts doing this "happy dance" in the front seat. This woman was in bumper to bumper traffic, putting on pantyhose! It took her about a quarter mile, but she succeeded. I admit I stayed behind her to watch because I was shocked that she was attempting to put on pantyhose in traffic. When she finished, I can honestly say that I pulled into the lane next to her and when she happened to look over at me, I gave her the thumbs up. Good job! I know for a fact I am not that talented although I can promise that I will never attempt to put on pantyhose in or out of traffic.

75

JOSE'S FAMILY VACATION

Now that you have read some of the odd situations I have encountered up until this point, let me throw another one at you. I was driving late at night when I got a call to pick up someone from the rideshare area at the airport. I was on the highway at the time which seems strange because if I got the request while traveling down the highway, it meant the rideshare queue at the airport was empty which is extremely rare. It took me 4 minutes to get to rideshare area A1 where Jose got into the truck without any luggage. I always find it odd to pick up a passenger who doesn't have any luggage and Jose was no exception because he had just returned from Thailand. I should also mention; Jose was traveling with his family.

To make a long story short, Jose lived about 14 minutes from the airport. I took Jose to his home where he then got into his minivan and returned to the airport to pick up his luggage and his family. I told Jose I could have taken all of them and their luggage to his house in one trip, but Jose told me he didn't mind. He had been in Thailand for a month which would have been a hefty parking fee at $11 a day in long-term parking.

I dropped Jose off and I headed back to the airport where I got another ride within minutes of my arrival. I am assuming Jose was right behind me in his minivan.

76

ROSEY'S INDECISION

When I received a ride request to pick up Rosey, I had no idea an hour of my time was about to be swallowed up like bullfrog eating a house sparrow. This ride took 63 minutes and I walked with $32. My patience was tested over and over again.

I picked up Rosey at the same bar where the I picked up the girl with the onions on her jumbo hot dog. Rosey and two of her friends got into the truck and told me they needed to get to Cook Out. Cook Out is a small burger place that has many locations around the Nashville area. I began heading to the address Rosey had entered into the rideshare app.

15 miles later, Rosey figured out she had put the wrong Cook Out address into the app. After she corrected it, we did a U-turn and headed back in the direction from which we had just come. When we arrived at the desired location, it was closed. However, Taco Bell next door was still open, making this the 3rd potential drop off point. There is nothing like a chicken quesadilla at 2 am. I waited in line for the trio's food for 10 minutes because 6 other people beat us to the drive-thru line. Rosey made the decision while we were waiting for her food that she would rather go to her mom's house, so she changed the drop-off point for the fourth time. After we finally got the trio their food, we headed for Rosey's mom's house

which was only 5 minutes away. The problem was that the other two people with Rosey didn't want to go to her mom's house.

So, when we got to mom's, Rosey got out and then changed the drop-off point for the fifth time. The fifth drop off location was 25 minutes away. I am not sure she realized that every time she changed the drop-off point the price went up. 25 minutes later and 50 miles later, I was on to my next call. Patience is a virtue worth $32 at 2 am.

77

SHANNA

Shanna got into the truck at 4:30 am. She got out of the truck at 4:48 am. Most of that time was spent waiting at red lights because I drove Shanna and her friend less than 2 miles. I picked up Shanna at the emergency room. She and her friend had gone out drinking on honkytonk row on Broadway in Nashville. They decided to drink so much that they got a ride to the hospital in an ambulance. My guess would be that they paid over $400 for the ambulance ride, but the ride to their house by an early morning rideshare driver only cost them $6. Drinking in Nashville can be expensive.

78

OTHER DRIVERS

Some of the best stories are told to me from riders I am taking to the airport. Usually, airport rides are longer than others and I get a chance to have better conversations with the passengers. Many of them comment about how clean my truck is compared to other vehicles. Some people tell me about their jobs. Some tell me about what airline they like the best. But then there are others who share stories about other drivers. I am always curious about other drivers because I know some of them are good, some are bad. Some of them are normal and some of them are not. The following stories are a few of the "nots".

Luke and his luck

I picked up Luke from his very large home and we headed to the airport. The ride was about 20 miles or so and we had a great conversation. Luke told me that he doesn't always have the best of luck with drivers.

For example, he took a rideshare in San Francisco. When he got into the vehicle, he began making small chat with the driver who informed Luke that he had recently moved to San Fran from the northeast to "make a change". Evidently, the driver suffered from some anxiety. Nothing could have prepared Luke for the answer. "Left turns" said the rideshare driver. Now I will say that a driver who is afraid of making left turns, SHOULDN'T BE DRIVING. Luke panicked when they were almost to his destination and the driver came upon a left turn. The driver started to sweat. "Just relax" blurted Luke, "I will get you through this! I promise". Luke said he felt like he was doing Lamaze training, forcing the driver to breathe over and over as he made the left turn. It was a close call, but Luke talked him through it. We can relax now.

Aliens among us

Another driver I heard about is one of those people who makes you scratch your head. One of my passengers asked the driver about people they drive to the airport. This driver in Minneapolis told the rider, "I pick up all kinds of people. Young, old, black, white, aliens, etc. You know the deal". "The deal" my rider asked? "Do you mean illegal aliens?" The driver went on, "no, you know what I am talking about. They're out there" he said with very wide eyes. The driver proceeded, "Did you know we sent a military unit to Afghanistan and they disappeared. So, the government secretly sent in paratroopers to find the missing unit. They found the remains of the missing unit and a creature that stood 8 feet tall, covered in hair, and had two mouths. They live among us and I have picked up a few here and there."

Keep in mind the guy telling the story is behind the wheel, authorized by his rideshare company to be driving others around town. I wanted to know if he had ever met E.T. or Chewbacca, but alas I was not there.

Aleena and her driver

I thought Aleena was a riot. She told me about a rideshare driver who took her and her friend to the airport a few months back. He had his radio set to volume 13, no more, no less. They asked him if he could turn up the radio when a song came on that Aleena really liked. "I can't do that; the radio needs to stay at level 13," said the driver. Level 13 it is.

HOWEVER, a few minutes later a song came on that the driver really liked. Without any forewarning, the driver cranked up the radio as loud as it would go. He started singing the song at the top of his lungs. Aleena and her friend sat back thinking, "What in the world is happening" as they looked at each other with strange faces. The driver sang that song as loud as he could and when it was over, the radio was set back to 13 and the ride continued. Aleena told me she sat there and didn't make sound and just looked forward until they arrived at the airport.

She said she hasn't ever been "that creeped out and confused at the same time" in her whole life. I told her, "there's a first for everything".

The driver with the stuffed animals

As I drive people all over this city, I hear stories about other rideshare drivers. I frequently get comments on the smell of my truck and the cleanliness of my truck. I hear horror stories about rideshare drivers who's car smells like pot or like hamburgers. I hear about the filth and grime some passengers must endure while driving to their destination at all hours of the night. Then I heard about this driver with stuffed animals on his dashboard. I didn't think much of it until another passenger told me the same story about this driver whose dashboard is covered with stuffed animals.

The story goes that when a passenger gets into this man's car, he asks you what stuffed animal you would like to hold for the duration of the ride. He then hands the passenger a stuffed bear or dog or whatever is in reach. Both girls who told me this story (on separate occasions) told me they were handed a teddy bear. They both said they were afraid to say, "No Thanks" and so they willingly held the bear until it was ready to jump out and run for the hills. I'm sure this driver means well, but he's creepy and I have a feeling if I ever see him, I will tell him about the creepy stories I have heard.

Kenny – worst rideshare driver ever.

I have to tell you about Kenny because he was so bad that I was inspired to write an entire section of this book called *Lessons Learned* as a way of telling drivers what they shouldn't do while on the job. This all began when I used my rideshare app to request a ride to the airport. I was leaving town for 5 days on business and it is cheaper for me to take a rideshare to and from the airport rather than parking in long term parking for that time.

I had two hours before my flight when I hit the *confirm request* button on the rideshare app. Within a few seconds, I received confirmation that Kenny was on his way and I could see his vehicle icon on the map on my phone. Kenny must have received my request as he was passing my exit because he drove 4 miles to the next exit and then 4 miles back to my exit which prolonged his arrival. This has happened to me, so I didn't think anything about it when it happened. Sometimes passengers have bad timing when making their request to no fault of their own. When Kenny finally arrived, it all went downhill from there.

First, I had a suitcase that needed to go into the trunk. Kenny popped the trunk when he arrived, but he didn't get out of his car to help me with my luggage. He just sat there like a lump on a log and waited for me to load my own luggage into his trunk that was full of crap. He had so much stuff in his trunk that if I would have had another suitcase with me, I doubt it would fit. I then got into the backseat and he says, "I guess you're going to the airport?" I was thinking to myself, "what gave it away Einstein?" He then told me he didn't really want to go to the airport again. I actually said to him, "if it's a problem, I can request a different driver." Note to drivers: when a passenger makes a comment like this, you have already lost any hope of getting a tip. Kenny replied that it wasn't my fault that he wanted to go to lunch and that he would take me to the airport. What a guy!

I had a hard time hearing anything Kenny said as we traveled to the airport because he had the radio turned up very loud. He wasn't listening to music; he was listening to political radio. I would never listen to political radio in my truck when I had a passenger in the truck because there is a 50/50 chance the passenger doesn't share my political views. Epic fail Kenny. You're batting zero so far.

I didn't tell Kenny that I was a fellow driver and I didn't tell him that I was writing a book. Instead, I used the time to do some research and perhaps find some best practices. Unfortunately, I didn't find any. Kenny asked me why I needed to go to the airport. I could have responded that I couldn't get southwest to fly me from my home, but instead, I told him that I was in the appliance business and I was going to be doing some consulting for a company who needed help in an area where I happened to be a subject matter expert. This was the truth. Kenny responded, "why does that require you to travel, can't you do that from home?" I was really getting the feeling that Denny didn't like going to the airport, what about you? Kenny then told me that he should have turned off his app because he was hungry and ready for lunch. He did this as he drove like a nut-ball down the highway, making lane change after lane change. He was zigzagging at top speed and for a moment I am sure I heard his stomach growl.

I asked Kenny if he ever drove at night and he responded, "shady people use rideshare at night" and so he only drove during the day. I must be shady because I drive at night and pick up all those shady people. I also asked Kenny if he could set his app so he only got rides that would keep him in the area where he liked to work? I asked him this knowing full well that the app has filters that can be set by the driver to only give them rides that take them in a certain direction such as to a given location or to their home. I use the filter to get rides to the airport when I am wanting to get back to the airport or that general vicinity. Kenny told me he had been driving for 3 years and he knew about some filters on the app but didn't know how to use them.

When we arrived at the airport, Kenny pulled up to the curb and popped the trunk. Then he said, "have a nice day." I got out, got my luggage out of the junk-filled trunk, and went into the airport. I am sure Kenny went straight to lunch. Even though he was a bit of a jerk, he gave me lots of material for my book. I would like to dedicate the lessons learned section of this book to Kenny.

79

LESSONS LEARNED

This section of the book is dedicated to lessons I have learned over the first 1000 rides I have completed with rideshare. Some lessons are geared toward drivers or those people who may think about becoming a rideshare driver in the future. Other comments are for passengers. I tried to keep this short, succinct, and funny. I also believe they apply to male and female drivers and passengers. They also apply no matter if the driver or passenger rides with Uber, Lyft, Zimride, Juno, Gett, Curb, Via, Wingz, or any of the other rideshare apps. One thing to always remember, you will never see it all. I hate the phrase "I will never see it all" because just when you say that, something else peculiar happens that makes your mouth drop to the floor. I never know who is going to get into my vehicle. They don't know me, and I don't know them. This is an important thing to remember. Every person is different and unique in their own way. I try not to judge people as they get into my truck, but to be honest, I judge them as soon as get out of my truck. Most people were good natured-although there were a few that I hope I never see again.

80
LESSONS LEARNED FOR DRIVERS

Take a bath

Something I think all rideshare drivers must do before you start your day is to take a bath or shower. There is nothing worse for a passenger to get into a car with a driver who smells. After the bath, use deodorant but leave the cologne in the cupboard. What the driver might find to be an alluring cologne, the passenger may want to vomit when smelling the same scent. A bath or shower should include lots and lots of soap and shampoo. Even if the driver is beginning his day at 2 am, a shower or bath should be mandatory before getting into the vehicle. If you smell, don't drive.

Dress for Success

The driver should always dress for success. When a passenger makes a ride request, they are basically hiring the driver for their ride. This means that drivers should wear clothes that are freshly laundered and should fit properly. In my opinion, hoodie sweatshirts should be outlawed for rideshare drivers. No passenger wants to get into a vehicle with a driver who has their hood pulled up over their head like a Jawa from Star Wars. Dressing or acting like a thug is horrible customer service. Drivers should wear something that they might wear when going to a job. I was at the airport earlier today and saw a guy get out of his LYFT XL wearing dress slacks, a white shirt, and a vest. I didn't think he was overdressed, in fact, I think he looked great. He drove like an ass, but he looked nice. I am not saying that a suit or tuxedo is appropriate, although that would be rather comical to pull up to a passenger in a little Toyota Prius wearing a tuxedo. Actually, skip that, it would be really creepy now that I think about it.

Clean your car

When a passenger rents a driver, they are also renting their vehicle. Therefore, the vehicle should be clean. I don't know how many people have hopped into my truck and commented that they are happy it doesn't smell like smoke or weed. It still baffles me that drivers smoke weed in their car and then go pick up passengers. Smoking is a disgusting habit. Drivers should know that just because they are standing outside their car, that doesn't mean the cigarette they are smoking isn't permeating their clothing, skin, and hair. When the driver gets back into their car, they may as well be using an ashtray air freshener. Also, people who smoke pot should NOT be driving for UBER, LYFT, or any other rideshare company.

Another comment about the vehicle, clean out the trunk. The trunk of the car should be completely empty. I can't tell you how many times I have requested a LYFT for a ride and when the driver arrived, the trunk was full of junk such that there was barely room for my suitcase. I see this often at the airport when I pull up behind other rideshare drivers. They pop the trunk to get the passengers suitcase and their trunk is full of stuff. I also see rideshare drivers in parking lots cleaning their windows, polishing their hubcaps, and wiping down the inside of their car. I think the cleanliness part of that situation is great, but the trunk shouldn't be full of cleaning supplies. The trunk is rented space that belongs to the passenger for the duration of their ride.

Music choices

I am continually changing the music I play when a passenger gets into the truck. The driver may have their own favorite music, but the passenger's choice is the only thing that matters. Drivers shouldn't be afraid to ask the passenger if they have a preferred type of music. If not, play something very soft and generic. I listen to XM radio and I try to prejudge the passenger's music choice when I pull up to the curb. If a guy is wearing a cowboy hat, I choose the country music station. If picking up a young person, I turn on "Today's Hits." When my parents get into my truck, I put on the oldies station. This isn't stereotyping, this is more of a calculated hunch. That being said, I still ask them if they have a preferred choice of music. Some passengers want to talk and so I simply turn off the radio.

Side note: The day after I wrote this paragraph, I picked up a passenger named Shira. She commented on the fact that I was playing Queen's Greatest Hits during her 18-minute ride. She said I was the coolest rideshare driver ever. Thanks, Shira!

Rich people and business travelers are the worst tippers

This is something I have found to be very consistent. Business travelers and rich people rarely tip so treat every passenger the same. I have heard stories about drivers being extra nice to people who they perceive have money. I am guilty of doing this myself and it almost never pays. I have found that treating everyone the same will yield tips that I could never imagine. Rides that I thought went very well, end up with no tip. Rides where the passenger never said a word, sometimes result in a very good tip. Sometimes a rider will even tip a driver with a bottle of wine, you never know.

Rideshare doesn't pay much money

If a driver takes the time to review any number of the bad tutorials that can be found online, the subject of earnings is always a topic of conversation. Every driver thinks they make more money than the next and all of them seem to think they have the secret formula in their town as to where to go and when to go. Generally, these drivers are full of themselves such as Mr. Moneybags. It is true that "surge" areas happen from time to time, but they don't last long. If a driver picks up someone in the surge area, chances are they will only get one or two rides in that surge area before the surge is over.

Drivers must pay maintenance on their vehicle and must buy their own gas. Vehicle wear and tear along with adding miles to the vehicle will ultimately reduce the value of the vehicle. The rideshare companies find ways to take more money from the driver. Some of them take a percentage followed up by an administrative fee. While rideshare is a good way to get some quick cash and it's a good hobby, I would never recommend it as a career. I would also recommend against the rideshare programs that give a driver a car in exchange for a certain number of rides each week. The driver is losing more than they are gaining.

Don't watch the driver Queue

Drivers will notice that during a ride, another passenger may be added to their queue. This means as soon as the first ride is finished, the driver is already on their way to the next passenger who is waiting. The problem is, the passenger in the queue can change many times during the first ride. I will see notices that say, "Seth has been added to the queue" and then 2 minutes later I will get a message that says, "Amanda has been added to the queue." What happened to Seth? Seth got another driver assigned to him that was closer than I was which is good for Seth. I have seen my queue change 5 times during the same ride, only to end the first ride and have no one waiting in the queue. Drivers should just ignore the queue until they are on their way to the next ride, keeping in mind that passengers can change while in route. I am sure most drivers have seen a situation where they thought they were on their way to pick up Seth but then given directions that change, ultimately leading them to Amanda. This happens frequently so drivers must always have one eye on the road and one eye on their app.

Listen more, talk less, but still talk

Drivers should spend more time listening to passengers. Talk to the passenger. Ask the passenger about their day, where they are heading, what airline they are using, etc. A good driver should feel out the situation. If a passenger isn't very talkative, then keep the conversation to a minimum. If the passenger is talkative, then talk to them.

Here are a few things drivers shouldn't do. First, don't drive the whole ride with a single passenger and never say a word. If you can't make conversation, don't drive. Customer service starts with a warm welcome and a good conversation starter. Second, don't bombard the passenger with questions. I had a driver pick me up from the airport who asked me 40 questions when I got into the vehicle. He asked about my destination, my music choice, the temperature of the vehicle, if my phone was charged, if I was tired, blah, blah blah blah blah. I think a few questions are good, but again, if the passenger isn't very talkative, leave the conversation to a minimum.

Third, drivers should never unload their life history and all their problems on the passenger. The passenger requested a ride from point A to point B. They did not request the driver's life story. I have heard horror stories from passengers who got into a rideshare vehicle and the driver just went off about their love life, their family life, their problems, their breakups, and heartaches, etc. The passenger will usually listen in a frightful, "get me the hell out of here" kind of way. The passenger doesn't care about the driver's issues, just get them to their destination.

Road Rage

Another thing I hear frequently from my passengers is how the last driver had road rage. Sometimes it is difficult to be on the road with idiots who make rather stupid choices such as bad lane changes, failing to abide by any traffic laws, and those who drive as if they own the road. This is especially bad at the airport drop off lanes. The general public loses their mind when they get behind the wheel. Some of them text, some eat oatmeal. I will admit that it is hard to not make comments or flip off those who do irritating things on the road. Nevertheless, the passenger should never witness road rage from the driver. Sadly, I hear this far too often. The other sad side note, it's very sad when the driver I am wishing I could flip off because they are driving like an idiot, turns out to be another rideshare driver who should probably be taking a bath and cleaning out their trunk rather than making illegal lane changes. I will say that if passengers want to express their distaste for idiot drivers along the route, more power to them.

The airport Queue

Depending on your city, the airport queue is an area where rideshare drivers go to wait for a passenger from the airport who needs a ride. This is a great way to waste time if you are not diligent in your planning. I see riders who spend all their time in the airport queue, waiting around while I am out getting ride after ride. In fact, a few weeks ago I had been to the airport 4 times with passengers in the morning and the same cars were still waiting in the rideshare lot. They always make me laugh. The airport queue is where I met Mr. Moneybags who wasted 90 minutes of his day waiting for a ride.

The airport queue can move fairly quickly at the end of the day when there are lots of flights landing at the airport. However, I wouldn't recommend sitting in the queue in the morning when people are coming to the airport. You do what's best for you, but I recommend only using that queue as a way of grabbing an easy ride at peak times. The rest of the time you are better off being out and about rather than sitting around doing nothing. I sat in the airport queue one time and will never do it again.

The right vehicle

What is the right vehicle to use for ridesharing? Some people will lead you to believe that you should only use a small vehicle that gets 400 miles to the gallon. Mr. Moneybags told me I wouldn't make any money if I didn't have a Prius. It turns out, Mr. Moneybags was an idiot – first class. The best vehicle you can use is a clean vehicle that doesn't smell like smoke, that has a completely empty trunk, and that can seat a minimum of 4 people. Anything larger than that will work just fine. Some drivers think that driving a truck is a bad idea. I will argue that driving a tiny car that gets good gas mileage is a bad idea. I can't tell you how many times I have heard horror stories from passengers who requested a ride and when the driver showed up, the passengers and their luggage didn't fit. You simply can't get 3 or 4 people and their large suitcases into a Toyota Prius or Honda Civic. If you do, the passengers will be very cramped and uncomfortable. This is no way to increase your tips. When I show up in my truck, I can fit as much luggage in the back which is always clean and covered with a tonneau cover. Passengers sit very comfortably in my truck and while it may take more gas, I make up for the extra gas with extra tips.

Obey the traffic laws

As a general comment, drivers in this city do not know the rules of the road. I know some people may be offended by that remark, but I hear it every day from passengers who tell me about other drivers they have had in this great city. It is a fact that driver's education is not required in Tennessee to get a license. The roads in this town are full of people who literally don't know basic traffic laws.

Drivers should know that stop signs are NOT optional! Stop means STOP. The vehicle should come to a complete stop. Coasting through a stop sign simply because no one else is coming, is not acceptable. Turn signals are very useful and should be used frequently. If a driver is making a lane change without using their turn signal, they should be slapped. Red lights between 12 am and 6 am are not optional. I am always amazed at how the general public in this town will pull up to a red light, look both ways, and then barrel through it like the Kool-Aid guy crashing through a wall. I have driven all over this country and using napkin math, I have driven over 400,000 miles in my life. I really enjoy living here, but driving in this city is downright scary. What is truly sad is how many rideshare drivers I see each day ignoring traffic laws. Passenger safety is paramount and therefore traffic laws should always be followed.

81
LESSONS LEARNED FOR PASSENGERS

The lessons for passengers are things passengers should know or take into consideration before they use rideshare. If a passenger wants to have a pleasant experience, it takes pre-planning and patience. Everyone is different and every driver is different. Passengers who have a preconceived notion in their head about what their rideshare experience will be like will most likely be disappointed. Passengers must be understanding and willing to overlook the fact that no driver is perfect, and no rideshare experience will be absolutely perfect every time. When you are dealing with the general public, you have to be flexible. As you read the lessons below, take note: every lesson is a result of dealing with passengers who don't think ahead and who take their driver for granted. If you read the advice and apply it when you are using a rideshare company, you will have a better experience and stand a better chance of being in a good mood when you get to where you are going because the driver will go out of their way to take care of you. When some of the things below happen, it puts me in a bad mood. I am less likely to go above and beyond for a customer who does some of the things listed below, just saying.

Plan your schedule

The passenger must always plan ahead. The driver is almost never going to be 2 minutes away unless you happen to be in a city or populated area and even then, it's hit and miss. Passengers must realize there are always a limited number of drivers and if a passenger needs a ride, chances are other passengers are also in need of a ride. I can't stand it when a passenger gets into the truck upset that they had to wait for a driver to show up. Drivers can't account for traffic, weather delays, construction delays, and the fact that they may be on the other side of town when the ride request is sent to them. Passengers should always allow themselves plenty of time when requesting a rideshare. If you are running late, it's not the fault of the driver. If you slept through your alarm, the driver is not at fault. If you are leaving the bar at closing time along with every other person in the area, it's not the driver's fault that other passengers made their request before you did. Riders should plan ahead. I always recommend, if a rider is downtown and the bars are about to close, it's better to leave early. It will be faster to leave the bar or club 15 minutes before closing and be the first to request a ride, rather than waiting and then standing around for an hour because all the drivers are on their way with passengers who beat you to the punch.

Drivers frequently change

The interesting thing about rideshare apps, the app will always try to pair up a rider with the driver who is closest to the rider. There are a few exceptions to this rule such as a rider who has downrated a driver. If a rider downrates a driver, that driver will not be paired with that passenger again. This can backfire on the passenger because if the only driver available is a driver who the passenger previously downrated, the passenger will have to wait for another driver; even if the driver is sitting around with nothing to do.

A passenger could be notified that I am their driver and I am on the way. However, the app can change and without warning, the passenger is notified that another driver is on the way. This could happen when another driver who is closer than I am logs on to the system and another passenger who is closer to me makes a request. The other driver will be given my rider and I will be diverted to the second person who made a ride request. Sometimes a passenger will be assigned to me, however nature calls. When I have to go to the bathroom, I will cancel a ride and thus the passenger will be given a different driver. Point is, these things happen. Don't get upset that the driver changed a few times before someone actually shows up to pick you up.

Message the driver

Sometimes a person will call a rideshare for a friend, family member or child. I would encourage anyone who is calling a rideshare for someone else, please message the driver so they know who they are picking up and who will be climbing into their vehicle. A good friend of mine was in Vegas for his grandson's 21st birthday. His name is Bud and he was staying at a hotel at the other end of the Las Vegas strip from where his grandson was staying. When his grandson called an UBER for Bud, the driver refused to take Bud to the hotel because the picture and name on the ride was not Bud but instead it was Bud's grandson. I see this frequently in this city. This morning I got a call to pick up Tiffanie at her home address. When I arrived, a young male walked up to the truck and climbed in. This was, in fact, Tiffanie's deadbeat son who overslept. He spent half the ride combing his hair although he should have spent the ride applying deodorant. This kid smelled like a hockey locker room. When this type of thing happens to drivers in the city, they have every right to refuse the ride for safety reasons. Therefore, if you schedule a ride for someone else, message the driver and let them know who they are picking up. This will save a lot of unnecessary hassles and headaches.

Gate codes and building numbers

When a passenger in an apartment complex requests a ride, always notify the driver of any gate codes or the building number where you are located. Some apartment complexes have multiple buildings, but the passenger uses the generic address of the complex. This doesn't help the driver at all because the driver has no idea what building in which the passenger is located. It will always be better to text the driver thru the app and let them know the building number where you are located so they have a better chance of finding you quickly. Also, if the apartment complex has a security gate, text the driver the gate code so they can easily gain access. I can't tell you how many times I have pulled up to an apartment complex with a closed gate. I have to then call the passenger and have them open the gate which takes time. On one occasion, I turned around and left. I didn't have the gate code and the passenger wasn't answering their phone. I tried to call two times and then I canceled the ride.

Where are you staying?

Similar to the building numbers and gate codes, always put the name of the hotel on a rideshare request. Hotels are usually found in groups and some of them can often share a parking lot. When making a ride request, the address is non-negotiable but it's always better to state the name of the hotel on the request. This will always help to expedite the ride because the driver will not have to take the time to attempt to figure out at which hotel they are supposed to go to pick up the passenger. I love it when a passenger puts the name of the hotel because I can see it from a distance away and I can choose alternative routes to get into the hotel parking lot if necessary. Also, the driver will have an easier time picking up the passenger from the front entrance. Some large hotels that have convention space such as the Gaylord Opryland Hotel in Nashville or some of the large hotels in Las Vegas, NV have rideshare "pickup areas." In this case, the driver can only pick up the passenger in the rideshare pick-up/drop off zone. The drivers are not allowed to pick up a passenger from any other area other than this designated zone, or they will get in trouble by the hotel. Passengers need to understand this because I have had situations where I arrived at the pick-up zone and the passenger was somewhere else. I waited the allotted time and then marked the passenger as a no-show which charged the passenger the no-show fee. If you are staying at a very large resort, ask the front desk if the hotel has a rideshare area. Again, it's not the driver's fault if you don't know.

Look for your ride, be there on time

The passenger should never request a ride until they are ready to go. A driver could take 2 minutes or 20 minutes to arrive. Passengers shouldn't make a request and then ask the driver to wait around because they got there quickly, and the passenger isn't ready to leave yet. I had a passenger request a ride and I arrived 5 minutes later. The passenger called me and told me they would be ready in 15 minutes. I waited 5 minutes and then left, which charged the passenger the no-show fee. The drivers time is valuable just as the passenger's time is valuable. It is not fair to the driver to request a ride and then expect them to wait around while you get ready to leave. If a ride is requested, the passenger should be ready and then be on the lookout for the driver to arrive.

The night I put this section on my list of things to talk about in this book, I was driving downtown in music city. I got a request to pick up Meredith from a honky-tonk bar on Broadway. I showed up and then waited around for 5 minutes. I called Meredith and spoke to her two times. She kept telling me she was on her way, but she never showed up. I ended up canceling the ride and got my $5 cancellation fee. Before I pulled away from the curb, I got another request from someone else at the same bar. The second rider was standing 20 feet from my truck. They jumped in and we were on our way. Amy wasted her money because she wasn't ready to go and wasn't looking for her ride when the ride showed up. Good for me, bad for her.

Smoking

Smoking is disgusting. If that statement offends you, then I am happy because I am offended anytime a smoker gets into my truck. I don't want my personal vehicle to smell like an ashtray and neither do all my other passengers. I don't understand why smokers think that if they stand outside and smoke, the smell will not be in their hair, skin, and clothing. Fact is, it will. If you smoke, you smell like smoke no matter what measures you take to attempt to disguise the smell. I say the same thing to drivers who smoke. Smokers will always smell like smoke. I keep 5 different kinds of air freshener in my truck and on many occasions, I am forced to drive to the next ride with all my windows down as I am attempting to get the foul smell of smoke out of my truck before I pick up the next passenger. If you are going to use rideshare, please do not stand around and smoke before your driver arrives. When I see a passenger throw down a cigarette before they get into my truck, I automatically dislike that passenger. I don't want to talk to them, I just want them out of my vehicle.

Adding stops along the route

To be honest, this is my biggest pet peeve with the whole idea of ridesharing. Nothing upsets me more than picking up a passenger who is going somewhere but puts stops along the way such as a gas station or fast food restaurant. The reason for my anger, the driver gets paid nothing extra to sit around and wait for their passenger to go into a gas station or fast food restaurant to buy whatever they need. Drivers lose money in the long run when they have to sit around at a passenger stop. This is a big waste of time for the driver. The drivers time is valuable, and time is money. The driver wants to take a passenger from point A to point B, drop them off, get paid, and then find another passenger. Waiting around while some high school student on their way to school is wasting time in Chick-Fil-A is aggravating at best. I only point this out because there is nothing stopping a passenger from putting in a stop along their route. However, passengers should know they are pissing off their driver which is never a good thing to do.

Don't eat in the car

One of the worst things a passenger can do is assume it's ok to eat in a rideshare vehicle. Don't even ask permission, just don't do it. Do you want someone that you don't know eating in your car? The passenger must realize that the vehicle belongs to the driver. The driver doesn't give the vehicle back to a company at the end of the day who is responsible for cleaning and maintenance of that vehicle. The vehicle is the driver's personal vehicle when they are not "on the clock." The passenger must also consider that when they get out and leave the vehicle, the smell of their food can linger which forces the driver to spray down their car with some type of air-freshener. Two times I have had people get into my truck with a hotdog that is covered in onions. There is nothing worse for a passenger than to get into a vehicle that smells like onions from the previous driver. Thankfully I always carry at least 3 types of air freshener in my truck. The bottom line, it's never ok to eat in a rideshare vehicle.

Car seats are required for small kids

This one always surprises me. The use of car seats for small children is the law in most states and it's not optional. Fines can run from $10 to $500 depending on the state. I don't understand why parents think the laws of the state do not exist if they take a rideshare. I also don't understand why a parent would put a small child's life at risk by letting them ride in a stranger's vehicle without a car seat. Of course, the drivers are just as much to blame as the passengers. Drivers should never allow a passenger with a small child without a car seat to enter their vehicle. The excuse that parents will use is that they do not want to lug a car seat around with them all day. This is a small price to pay for the safety of their child. Lazy parents who are willing to put their child's life in danger shouldn't be parents. I have turned down rides for parents for this reason. I drive up, they have a small kid, I ask about their car seat and if the answer is no, then they don't ride in my vehicle. Don't attempt to take a rideshare with a baby or small child under the age of 12 without a car seat. End of story.

Don't slam the door

The door of the vehicle in which you are riding never hurt you, so why are you trying to hurt it by slamming it shut when you exit the vehicle? Sadly, this happens every day. Every day someone gets out of my truck and feels the need to slam the door as hard as they can. I wish my door would slam them back. There is no reason for it. Again, passengers should treat the vehicle as they would want their vehicle treated. There is no need to pop my eardrums out of their sockets by slamming the door.

Make the driver cancel the ride if their car is too small.

I know this one is going to upset the rideshare drivers, but this advice is the best advice a passenger should take away from reading this book. Make the driver cancel the ride. Here is how it works: if the passenger cancels the ride after the driver is on site, the passenger must pay a cancellation fee. I am a big believer in cancellation fees for passengers who cancel the ride at the last minute. Passengers can't expect to request a rideshare, run the driver from one side of the town to the other, cancel at the last minute, and then leave the driver high and dry. In fact, I think cancellation penalties should be higher than they are at this time.

That being said, if a driver arrives in a tiny car and the passengers or the luggage will not fit, passengers should ask the driver to cancel the ride. It's no secret that I drive an F150 the majority of the time when I am out picking up passengers. The best thing about my truck is that there is plenty of room in the bed of the truck for luggage. I have no problem picking up a family of 4 and all their luggage as they are heading to the airport.

Most of the rideshare drivers with these tiny cars with junk in the trunk can't say the same. I have heard many times where a passenger had to request a different rideshare driver because the first on-site couldn't fit all the people and their bags into their car. When this happens, the fault is on the driver, not the passenger. Therefore, if the driver has a tiny car whereas the passengers and their luggage will not fit, force the driver to cancel the ride to avoid unnecessary cancellation fees.

Rideshare drivers are weird

Now that you have read the majority of this book and this section of learned lessons, there are a few final lessons to realize before taking a rideshare. The fact is, most drivers are strange in some way, shape or form. I never said I wasn't strange; in fact, my family would tell you just the opposite. I mention this because taking a rideshare can be aggravating and even creepy at times because all of us are different. You will rarely find a perfect driver who does everything you want them to do, plays the perfect music, and has a perfect car in which you can't find some fault. Some drivers talk to themselves; others talk to you when you don't feel like talking. Some of them have road rage, some of them smell, and some of them talk to aliens. You have to expect this and laugh it off when it happens. I make light of the situation and you should too. Look at your driver as a form of entertainment for the ride. Even if you're laughing at them or rolling your eyes without them seeing, at least they showed up and are taking you to your destination.

Don't downrate your driver

Think twice before downrating your driver. Your bad day or perception of what you think should be a perfect ride is no excuse to judge someone harshly. Rideshare drivers are out there making a living and they are doing their best to get you from your current location to your destination. You called them because you don't have a car, or you don't have use of a vehicle or you simply don't want to drive. They are doing the work so remember that before you rate a driver below a 5. Riders should be reminded that a driver can downrate a rider as well. If a rider's rating falls to a low level, the rideshare company can deactivate the account of the rider just like they could deactivate a driver.

Everyone should ask themselves how they feel when they get a review at work and get blindsided by their boss. It's no fun to get a bad review when you think you did everything ok. This is the same for the driver. They may have provided a good ride to all their passengers during a given week and so it's disappointing when their weekly review is sent to them via email only to find that a few passengers downrated them. The only driver I have ever downrated is a jerk who had an attitude about using a car seat. I don't want someone in my truck who wants to be a pain in the ass when it comes to the safety of their child. Rate your driver a 5.

Tip your driver

Last but not least, give your driver a tip. They earned it. If you are the type of person who will have a server in a restaurant wait on you hand and foot but then you leave them nothing, then I can tell you that I don't like you. I always tip, even if I have had a not so good ride. Even if you only leave them $1, you are still giving your thanks for the work they did getting you from point A to point B. Drivers don't get paid to wash their car or ensure their car has gas to get you where you are going. Drivers must get up early and be out in the area where you need them. They make a lot of effort for every passenger that the passenger never sees. They must use restraint when dealing with construction areas or jack-hole drivers. They also must maintain their vehicle in every way. For these reasons, give your driver a tip and let them know that you not only appreciate the ride, but you appreciate their other efforts to ensure you can get to your destination. My ultimate goal: to get cash or a box of donuts as a tip at the end of a ride, although I still appreciate the bottle of wine.

82

LOGGING OFF FOR THE DAY

So there you have it. Your first glance into the world of rideshare in Music City. It's not glamorous and doesn't pay well, but there is never a dull moment in the day and life of an Uber or Lyft driver. There is also never a shortage of rides to be found at all hours of the night. This is a party city. People come to Nashville to drink and listen to music. It doesn't matter if visitors and locals are in town to celebrate festivals, concerts, or even the NFL Draft of 2019. Drunk people, police stories, and airport adventures will continue every day of the year.

I want to reiterate a piece of advice to the readers: tip your driver. The driver has to deal with the drunks, the police, the traffic, and the headaches that come with the job. They are always around to pick up a needy passenger and get them to their destination. They must keep their car clean, refrain from road rage, they get little sleep at times, and they must always have a positive attitude. Granted, some of them smell, some don't speak English, and some are weird on many levels. That being said, they are still there to help passengers. Help them in return.

About The Author

Archie C. Edwards lives outside Nashville, Tennessee and has completed more than 1700 rideshare rides. He holds a Bachelor of Science degree in Education from The Pennsylvania State University and is currently working on his master's degree in Business Administration. He also holds many certifications in the appliance industry where he has worked for the last 16 years. He is an accomplished singer, performer and at times can be found playing piano at the occasional funeral.

People are just dying to hear him perform!

Printed in the United States
By Bookmasters